The One-Eyed Cat and the Gambler

A Collection of Aphorisms and Parables

by Jeffery Thorn Bennett

Dorrance Publishing Co
585 Alpha Drive
Suite 103
Pittsburgh, PA 15238
Visit our website at www.dorrancebookstore.com

ISBN: 979-8-89027-035-1
eISBN: 979-8-89027-533-2

Aphorisms

Time and Memory

*Time and memory are true artists; they remold reality
nearer to the heart's desire. John Dewey*

*It's a poor sort of memory that only works backwards. Lewis Carroll, Through
the Looking-glass*

1. Time n. a subjective illusion with the fraudulent ability to heal wounds

2. Time is nothing more than many discrete moments imagined as one.

3. Memory, not time, heals some wounds–a bad memory that is.

4. We are lucky if time leaves our wounds unscathed let alone heals them.

5. When one wastes time and regrets it, one pays double for a commodity not procured.

6. Our perceptions of past, present and future are merely arbitrary demarcations along a continuum, such perceptions being the subtlest of illusions.

7. The quality and character of present experience are determined by our choice of attitudes toward past events and future possibilities.

8. Time passes slowly for those who fancy themselves immortal but much too quickly for those who don't.

9. The present wishes to recapture what the past took for granted.

10. The attempt to recapture the past is the folly which despoils the present.

11. Nostalgia is often a longing for how things could have been rather than how they were.

12. While we may recollect the past or contemplate the future, we are forced to live in the present, an odd amalgamation of the aforementioned activities.

13. One's perception of time mirrors one's age and belief in immortality.

14. Eternity is the voice which silences Time while showcasing the beauty of a dying flower.

15. Future n. that which would be what everyone wants it to be if only it ever came to be

16. Past n. that which, like a thief in the night, steals away with the present

17. Present n. the chimera of memory's illusions

18. Infinity n. that which goes on and on and on, such goings on driving home the futility of going on with no end in sight

19. The smallest moments ignored in the moment may later move us the most.

20. Transience n. life swallowed by Eternity

21. Lost Souls phr. humanity adrift in the belly of Infinity

22. Nostalgia n. a longing for a sliver of the past restrained by present commitments

23. The Passage Of Time phr. Nature's last laugh at the expense of the young

24. Spring n. a paradoxical reminder of the transience of beautiful things gone forever.

25. Winter n. a welcome reminder of beautiful things yet to come.

26. Better to live in the past or the future than to be discontent in the present.

27. Wonder at the most trivial of things leads to wonder of the Infinite.

28. Sic Transit Gloria Mundi: Thus passes away the glory of the world–a warning unheeded by kings, writers and other fools who take their accomplishments too seriously

29. Tempus Fugit: Time flies–a maxim which makes the young scoff and the old recoil.

30. The moment is all that matters, but upon the moment it is impossible to dwell.

31. Memory n. the faculty whose primary function is to steer us into the unknown based on its misrembrances of the past

32. Memory pervades the present and is the source of such happiness and sorrow as we are likely to know.

33. Experience is only valuable when considered from the clear perspectives of memory and reflection, these two requirements being rare and mostly incompatible.

34. Memory limns the world as it never was; hope foresees it as it will never be.

35. Life is like fiction: tragic and comedic; we have our memory to thank for that.

36. A glorious future is the illusory projection of a bad memory.

37. Life is memory, never forget that.

38. What a bad memory cannot heal should never be left to the mercy of a good one.

39. Memories are like good friends. They'll tell you a compassionate lie when you need it the most.

Happiness

Some cause happiness wherever they go; others whenever they go.
Oscar Wilde

40. Happiness is mostly found in memory, and memory is mostly wrong.

41. Happiness is having a cat, especially one who ignores you. I once had such a cat, and I needed nor wanted anything else.

42. Happiness never gains a foothold, for it is either the apprehension of sorrows yet to come or the expectation that current sorrows are about to end.

43. Happiness cannot exist, for if it were ever attained it would be long gone before it could be recognized.

44. Happiness n.
  - the ultimate state energetically sought only to be had in the seeking
  - the misperception that the goal is preferable to the means
  - an ignis fatuus promised by ancient philosophers with too much time on their hands
  - schadenfreude
  - that which sometimes exists in the memory, never in the present and always in the future
  - a state of unrelieved boredom endured in heaven
  - an impossible demand which the present makes on the future

Knowledge and Wisdom

To attain knowledge, add things everyday; to attain wisdom, remove things everyday.
Lao Tse

45. Be careful that what you claim to know is not vitiated by insidious falsehoods.

46. Those who think critically about their own intelligence will immediately be impressed by its fallibility, an impression which, if widely held, would do the world much good.

47. Great harm is done in the world by those who believe much but know little, but those who know little sometimes know much of importance.

48. What one knows in relation to what is known is unworthy of mention, and what one knows in relation to what can be known is infinitesimal; in the realm of epistemology, arrogance is stupidity.

49. Those who know the least are sometimes the wisest; and those know the most are sometimes the biggest fools.

50. What I once thought I knew, I now believe to be absurd; what I now think that I know will doubtless befall the same fate. The truth stays a step ahead of belief.

51. Skeptic n. one who professes to know nothing while laboring to prove that no one knows anything.

52. Do not go to others for wisdom and insight; of the former, they likely have none; as to the latter, yours is likely as good as theirs.

53. The "I" is the source of all our actions, but the "I" is unknowable, perhaps just a fiction, and so alas are the properties of its actions.

54 Ideas which at one time were considered heretical to doubt are at a later one consigned to the dustbin of the archaic and peculiar, their residence there serving as a dusty reminder to the silliness of prevailing wisdom.

55. Omniscient adj. characterizing one who knows everything but sees nothing

56. Much of what passes for knowledge is guessing, and most guessing is arrogance.

57. Wisdom always involves enlightenment; knowledge seldom does.

58. Wisdom and Knowledge conj phr. the principal antagonists in the war between truth and power, wisdom being the perennial loser

59. Sixth Sense phr. yet another conduit for feeding ignorance

60. Unknown adj. describing all that is extremely important

61. Ignorance n. a dark hole in the soul spawning cruelty and the persecution of the innocent

62. To ask the unanswerable is an invitation to a fool's game politely declined by the wise.

Thought, Language, and Mystery

What can be said at all can be said clearly, and what we cannot talk about we must pass over in silence. Ludwig Wittgenstein, Tractatus Logico-Philosophicus

One of the hardest things in life is to convey a meaning accurately from one mind to another.

Lewis Carroll

63. Thought n. a slave of language nevertheless subject to improvement by a mastery of its master.

64. Thought cannot transcend language. That which is most important cannot be said.

65. Language n. a factitious constraint on wisdom and spawner of many fictitious constructs such as time, free will, personality, et. al.

66. Language imprisons thought; a sense of mystery disenthralls it.

67. Language straight-jackets thought and so leads ineluctably to skepticism.

68. What lies behind mystery cannot, of course, be expressed, but it can enthrall and inspire.

69. Mystery has two senses: that which is not known but may be discovered and that which it is impossible to know. The former is science; the latter is poetry.

70. Mystery loves a contradiction; the intellect abhors it.

71. The statement of a contradiction, carefully worded, may be a powerful impetus toward the truth.

72. Paradox is unlike mystery in that while both may profoundly affect our lives, paradox vexes the mind, mystery the soul.

73. Mystery, not logic, is the best argument for the existence of God; but mystery discloses nothing; it is, after all, mystery.

74. Those who embrace the incomprehensible may be closer to the truth than we suspect.

75. Wonder n. dumbfounded but awed by the unanswerable

76. Mystic n. one whose studied silence hides either sagacity or stupidity, the answer to which being of no great consequence, especially to the mystic

77. The mind cannot know what words cannot capture.

78. My thoughts are constrained by my place in time. I can only hope that quiet reflection will loosen these bonds.

79. From the penetralia of my mind arise those thoughts which perplex me most, the darkest of which I would fain disown.

80. 'Fascist' n. a term currently applied by those, with no knowledge of it meaning, to those with political views contrary to their own

81. 'Racist' n. another widely used term misapplied in the same way as the preceding

82. Succinctness n. the virtue of a good writer having something to say or the decorum of a bad one with the good sense not to offend

83. Ambiguous n. designating an expression presenting many opportunities for misinterpretation

84. Ambiguity is the heart of language and the essence of misunderstanding.

85. Thinking may be hard work but hard workers seldom think.

86. Idioms n. popular platitudes seamlessly transferred from one generation to the next, ensuring that one will know no more than the other.

87. Euphemism n. a saccharine expression invariably more offensive than the one it is supposed to supplant

88. Well Turned Phrase phr. an expression having more power to convince than a thousand cogent arguments

89. Clever adj. having the power to persuade when having nothing of substance to say

90. Clear adj. easily refuted

91. Cryptic adj. avoiding confutation by a masterful use of equivocation

92. Second Thought phr. a prelude to an even more pointless third thought

93. After Thought phr. the realization that what one has thought should never have been said

94. Style n. that which convinces when content cannot; see 'clever'

95. The style in which something is said may pique thought and creativity more than the substance of what is said.

96. Style adds a flourish to all that has ever been said, to all that can be said.

97. Most communication between individuals is bodily, a language of unspoken gestures in which most are not versed and thus find themselves at the mercy of its more careful readers.

Common Sense and Conventional Wisdom

Our prejudices are so deeply rooted that we never think
of them as such but call them common sense.
George Bernard Shaw

98. Common Sense phr. a type of sense altogether too common and much over-esteemed

99. Conventional Wisdom phr. the voice of those who think not for themselves but would silence the voice of those who do

100. Common Sense and Conventional Wisdom phrs. the ascriptions one makes to one's views when evidence cannot be found for their truth

101. Beware those who are forever citing common sense and conventional wisdom for their views, for they are the ones clearly afflicted by both.

102. Small minds are the handmaidens of common sense and conventional wisdom.

103. Nonsense n. a type of sense appreciably superior to her mother, common sense

104. Of all fears, the fear of conventional wisdom is the most craven.

105. Turn prevailing opinion upon its head and you will become wise, or at least not a fool.

Religion, Sin and Ritual

Religion n. A daughter of hope and fear explaining to ignorance the nature of the unknowable. Ambrose Bierce, The Devil's Dictionary

Religion is like a blind man looking in a black room for a black cat that isn't there, and finding it. Oscar Wilde

106. Religion n. a phase through which most people pass on the road to material pleasures and to which they return prodded by the fear of death

107. Agnostic n. one who takes a circuitous route to the truth; one lacking the courage of any conviction

107. Agnosticism n. a state of ignorance approaching wisdom; the phobia of being wrong or, as may otherwise be argued, a fealty to the truth

108. Atheist n. one who desires what he seeks to disprove; an agnostic gone to seed

109. God n. a being acting in mysterious ways when things go against one's prayers but in perfectly intelligible ones when things go as one had petitioned; all in all, a most accommodating chap

110. God may take many forms or none at all. Therefore, that God should exist is as worrisome a proposition as its opposite.

111. The silence of God toward the unalloyed evils of the world is telling.

112. Amidst the sorrows of the world, the subtlest manifestations of God elude great intellects and are perhaps best read by souls pure and simple.

113. Tears n. that which are shed for the loss of a loved one; for some, a powerful proof of the existence of God

114. Constellation n. one of God's quilts

115. The innocent die before God in the icey vastness of emerald silence.

116. Devil n. a wily fellow adept at stealing souls and frightening the innocent; a fabrication of the guilty

117. Original Sin phr. the ultimate wrongdoing originating in the Fall and for which those extant millenia later must atone; a phenomenon remarkable for its longevity

118. Deadly Sins phr. the sins which came later for the enlightenment of those who missed the point the first time

119. Gluttony n. a state of happy satiety and prominent member of the sin fraternity

120. Sloth n. a life of ease and luxury led by kings and the wealthy and envied by those who must work for a living

121. Envy n. an insatiable longing for the belongings of others, such others being afflicted by the same desire

122. Wrath n. the thrashing one desires to give to others for affronts both real and imagined, mostly imagined

123. Lust n that which, when satisfied, leads to sloth

124. Greed n. having much more than one needs and much less than one wants

125. Pride n. the deadliest of sins widely presumed to go before a fall but more often preceding a rise in the envy of popular opinion

126. The heavens express murkily what words cannot even suggest.

127. Religious belief succumbs to the confidence of youth only to undergo a cowardly redivivus in the frailty of old age.

129. Hell n. a place to which the wicked descend to be with others of like minds and predilections, a not altogether unpleasant destination

130. Heaven n. a realm of unrelieved boredom reserved for God's elect but happily shunned by reprobates, wags and those with joie de vivre

131. Soul n. a fantastic, incorporeal entity invented by humans to assuage worldly sorrow by encouraging the expectation of a blessed afterlife; a strange entity found only in humans, much to the delight of the higher animals

132. Faith n. that which, after a losing joust with logic, gains in arrogance; a sore loser
  • a belief without evidence as told by those without knowledge, about things without parallel Ambrose Bierce, The Devil's Dictionary
  • Proof is different than faith. The former is human; the latter is a gift from God. Blaise Pascal Pensées
  • Faith is believing what you know ain't so. Mark Twain, Following the Equator

133. Sky n. a vast shroud blocking our understanding but suggesting the divinity of the unknown

134. Polytheist n. one who, dissatisfied with one god, invents many in the hope of appeasing them all; a people pleaser taking it up a notch

135. Omniscient adj. characterizing one who knows everything but sees nothing

136. Omnipotent adj. characterizing our almighty but disinterested creator

137. Sacrilegious adj. characterizing the tenets of a religion other than one's own; evoking the ire of the faithful and the understanding of God

138. Prevent but one act of cruelty and raise yourself to divinity.

139. Worship v. to prostrate oneself before an inferior or nonexistent being.

140. The Last Judgment phr. the day on which we shall all be called to account for our actions, a day just like any other

141. Miracle n. a fortunate and improbable occurrence wrought daily by Nature; divine intervention given its undeserved due

142. Keep company with the lost and soar with angels.

143. Guardian Angels phr. divine beings asleep on the job.

144. Reincarnation n. a peculiar theory of the afterlife where those who come after jettison all memories and traces of having lived before; almost certainly, a case of mistaken identity

145. Freedom Of Religion phr. free from any inclination towards enlightenment.

146. There But For The Grace of God Go I: God's grace lavished on the wicked

147. Heathen n. one not yet exposed to the tyranny of religion

148. Buddhist n. one recognizing the futility of desire while desiring its opposite, the extinction of the pulse of life

149. Twilight n. a strange interlude between day and night soothing the soul and firing the imagination; an argument, as good as any, for the existence of God

150. Savior n. one who offers a service, usually for a fee, to souls rarely in need of the gesture but with heads ripe for a scalping.

151. Angels and demons may fight for your soul; make sure that it's worthy of their struggles.

152. Manichaeism n. a religious doctrine holding the world is governed by two equally powerful forces, good and evil, light and dark; the corollary of this view being that in the struggle between good and evil, there is no winner

153. To endure one's greatest misfortune one is prone to invoke the divine or the theurgical, a feckless attempt given that both are unlikely to exist or at best not to care.

154. Damnant Quod Non Intellegunt: They condemn what they do not understand—a maxim applicable to the world's religions and their detractors

155. Deus Operatum In Viis Arcanum: God works in mysterious ways–an affront to God and mystery

156. Funeral n. a barbaric ritual conducted by a priest, usually in a hurry, commemorating one, often a rogue, to satisfy attendees, impatient for dinner

157. Eulogize v. to lie with impunity and the imprimatur of the church

158. De Mortuis Nil Nisi Bonum: About the dead say nothing but good–lie profusely; see 'eulogize'

159. Deo Non Fortuna phr. by God, not luck–by caprice, not endeavor

160. Latitudinarian n. one who, knowing little about most religions, accepts them all; a mushhead afraid of offending anyone

161. Both faith and reason provide the comfort of psychological certitude and an unobstructed path to error.

162. Piety n. a service, usually a sacrifice, offered to a god, usually indifferent, intended as an appeasement, always ineffective; a prayer recited by rote blessing a sumptuous feast

163. Prayer n. a trite supplication offered when science and reason offer no hope; an appeal too easily offered on behalf of those in need of a more roborant gesture

164. Confession n. another benighted custom in which one begs absolution for a sin, probably never committed, from a priest, probably addled, governed by a superior hoping for a generous tithing, hardly affordable

165.Communion n. more ritualistic claptrap in which the communicants play the role of vampires

166. Lord's Prayer phr. a prayer composed by adults to ensure the obedience of children, their terror of God and a lasting allegiance to religious chicanery

167. The Father, The Son and the Holy Ghost conj. the holy trinity yoked together as one; acontradiction unquestioned by the faithful and resignedly accepted by those too fearful to object

168. Baptism n. the most of odious of religious rites in which an infant, possessing no will of its own, is initiated into a cult by its parents gleefully condemning others to Hell

169. Pope n. in the Catholic faith, the supreme official who interprets passages not found in the Bible or, when found, are perfectly comprehensible to simple-minded followers in need of reassurance from a higher source

170. Sainthood n. a lofty status granted by the Church to those it deems exceptionally holy and to have performed a miracle, the most common miracle being its belief in such holiness

171. Fideist n. one who, incapable of proving God's existence, turns the matter over to an incompetent ally, faith; a lazy believer

172. Deism n. a quasi philosophical theory envisioning God as the artificer of many worlds, this one being more the product of a detached tinkerer

173. Fideism n. reason, having failed in its divine mission, descending into faith

174. Blessed v. favored by either God or chance, the two being impossible to distinguish and of no material difference to those so favored

175. Heaven Sent phr. See 'blessed'

176. Credo Ut Intelligam phr. a famous saying of St. Anselm's translated as: I believe in order that I may understand—putting the divine cart in front of the proverbial horse

177. Parishioner n. one whose knowledge of the holy works derives mostly from the priest whose knowledge derives mostly from other priests

178. Afterlife n. the life which is eagerly awaited by the downtrodden and happily postponed by the fortunate

179. Prophet n. one who, claiming infallibility, proliferates the decrees of a being, supposedly divine, to followers begging to be led

Politics, Government and Society

That government is best which governs the least.
Henry David Thoreau, Civil Disobedience

180. Capitalist n. one who, after acquiring great wealth, acquires a license to steal

181. Plutocrat n. one who advocates rule by the wealthy; see 'capitalist'

182. Socialist n. one with a predilection for redistributing wealth other than one's own; a capitalist manque; knave

183. Communist n. one who, having no property to share, adopts the "what's yours is mine" philosophy; and, after successfully executing it, becomes a capitalist

184. Anarchist n. one who advocates for the destruction of society while enjoying its privileges and protection; one who sees the value of hypocrisy in achieving one's ends

185. Utopia n. an ill-conceived society envisioned by academicians and empty- headed idealists, the two being interchangeable

186. Dystopia n. the usual state of affairs, accepting uncomplainingly by realists and groused about by those mentioned above

187. Good Government phr. an oxymoron placidly accepted by the governed

188. Citizen n. an individual possessing certain inviolable rights voidable at the whim of the State

189 Property Is Theft: the clarion call of anarchists having no property to be stolen and no mind to be found

190. Society n. a network of covenants between the rich, the poor and the government, always favoring both the former and the latter

191. Liberal n. the antithesis of the conservative, both being the antithesis of reason and goodwill

192. Culture n. the fictitious construct of do gooders intent upon reinventing it in their own image

193. Democracy n. an irrational gamble on the intellect and goodwill of the elected

194. Participatory Democracy phr. an ancient form of democracy where each citizen, at various times, participates in making critical governmental decisions

195. Representative Democracy phr. A recent and one-sided form of democracy in which an electorate, woefully uninformed and indifferent, chooses leaders savvy and self-interested; natural selection working overtime in the political sphere

196. Ochlocracy n. rule by the mob; see 'participatory democracy'

197. Plutocracy n. rule by the rich; see 'capitalism'

198 Hagiocracy n. rule by priests, usually rich, for the good of the laity, invariably poor; a divine plutocracy

199. Autocracy n. a type of society ruled by a petty dictator, deficient in brains but possessed with an infallible instinct for seizing the moment and gauging the susceptibility of the herd

200. Meritocracy n. a type of society abhorred by socialists and others who take a reverent view of the property–mediocrity–essential to advance in public office

201. Libertarian n. one who espouses the "liberty is the summum bonum" philosophy; that is, a former paternalist having been ousted from a high governmental position

202. Paternalist n. one who champions the "government knows best" philosophy; that is, an ex libertarian having procured high office

Freedom and Free Will

Man, what are you talking about? Me in chains? You may fetter my legs but my will, not even Zeus can overcome. Epictetus, Discourses

None are so hopelessly enslaved as those who falsely believe themselves to be free.
Johann Wolfgang von Goethe

-

203.   Free Will phr. a necessary fiction by which we extoll some actions and condemn others, such contrivance being the linchpin of uncivilized societies

204. We do not freely choose our nature, our predilections, our dislikes; the same is likely true of our actions.

205. Our apprehension of free will is simply the awareness of a subjective impression and is as unlikely to be true as any such impression.

206. While we may have freedom from external constraint, free will is an illusion borne of wishful thinking.

207. Freedom n. a distant cousin of free will peculiar to nations with a love for human dignity, in every way as rare as its relative

208. Fatalism n. the view that whatever happens is preordained; a fine theory for those wishing to pass the buck when things don't go as they had planned

209. Free Thinker phr. one with the gall to question the entrenched views of society and science, the two being indistinguishable; see, Socrates, Galileo, Newton, et. al.

210. Will Power phr. the power of circumstance in protecting a weak will from harmful impulses

211. Look inward, look deep and find the stranger who dwells within; for he would propel you against your will.

Life and Death

We write to taste life twice, in the moment and in retrospect. Anais Nin

*Death is nothing to us, since when we are death has
not come, and when death has come, we are not.
Epicurus, "Letter to Menoeceus"*

212. Death n. a specter haunting both those who believe in immortality and those who don't; a prospect understood by none but feared by all

213. In the face of death, one may recoil, seek enlightenment or embrace what one believes is to come. It is perhaps best to do nothing.

214. While immortality could take many forms or none at all, it is unlikely to take the form for which one wishes.

215. Life n. that which is clung to with a tenacity which exposes the dread of its opposite

216. Life is a loose and peculiar concatenation of episodes, many considered by its successor to have been pointless and only nostalgically discovered later, but much too late, to have been priceless

217. Black Depression phr. life cowering in the shadow of death.

218. Boredom n. a myopic state curable by gin

219. The richness of opportunities not seized haunts us until our dying day.

220. Good Life phr. that which comes too quickly to an end; that type of life hopelessly
 intertwined with it opposite

221. The events of life have meaning, but life itself has none.

223. Meaning Of Life phr. a type of meaning in no mood to be grasped

224. Gone But Not Forgotten phr. having died a debtor

225. The Hereafter phr. existing in the here but never in the after

226. We all die alone, specks on a dark shore, cloaked in terrifying black clouds.

227. Eulogies are for the living, the living who prosper from saying fine things about the dead, fine things never thought truly but now being said.

228. The dead sleep well, and their grossest misdeeds won't send them to Hell.

229. Deed n. an action, good or evil, soon to be drowned in the leaden river of death

230. The meaning of life does not stray far from the mundane pleasures of ordinary existence. Have at least one fine dinner with friends before you die.

231. Memento Mori: Remember death–a sharp reminder, usually in the form of an artwork, that Death, bless His heart, will never forget about you

232. Mors Vincit Omnia: Death conquers all–a platitude denied by the young and the vain

233. Sic Transit Gloria Mundi: thus passes away the glory of the world– a warning unheeded by kings, writers and other fools who take their accomplishments too seriously

234. There is no ambit between life and death, no discrete moment upon which we can place a finger or reflect.

235. Nothingness n. the most dreaded of the possible ends to life; the incomprehensible opposite of somethingness

Morality and Justice

Moral indignation is jealousy with a halo.
H.G. Wells, The Wife of Sir Isaac Harman,

236. Morality n. a fine thing except in the hands of tyrants, zealots, and the self-righteous; that is, a thing rarely encountered; a deadly weapon when in the wrong hands

237. Injustice n. a scale weighted against the weak and the poor, such groups being too oppressed to counter the direction of the tilt

238. Justice n. a balancing of the scales in favor of my interests

239. There is no injustice so great that it retribution cannot be effected by kind hearts and clear heads, or powerful weapons newly acquired by the aggrieved.

240. Good and evil are polar opposites, but what lies in between and above should perplex us the most.

241. Golden Rule phr. a principle perhaps better described using a more prosaic mineral

242. Conscience n. the moral equivalent of bad judgment

243. Common Good phr. a hopelessly vague expression usually cited by those about to have their interests thwarted by another; the what I want is what you should do philosophy run amuck in the moral sphere

244. Immoral n. offensive to the bad taste of others

245. Mores n. that body of a society's principles posing as morality

246. Treat Everyone With Respect And Dignity: The foremost law ot the philosopher Immanuel Kant–a testament to the power of reason when freed from the shackles of emotion

247. Social Justice phr. the noble folly of trying to override the Law of Natural Selection

248. The Law of Natural Selection phr. a law which, when opposed by a well meaning society, ensures that the strong will grow stronger at the expense of the weak

249. Help Others In Need: a fine principle deriving from both the heart and reason

250. Assuage the misery of others and forfend sorrow to yourself.

251. Ten Commandments phr. moral prescriptions variously interpreted by varying religions each with the unvarying end of securing its fair share of very gullible adherents

252. I Am The Lord, Thy God, Thou Shall Have No Other Gods Before Me: God's unintended admission of His insecurity

253. Thou Shall Not Covet Thy Neighbor's Wife: the Ninth Commandment notable for failing to replace 'covet' with 'bake cookies with'.

254. **The Fourth Decalogue** phr. an unnecessary injunction to those who, having spent six days in debauchery, are too tired to labor on the seventh

Professions and Professionals

Philosophy n. a route of many roads leading from nothing to nowhereAmbrose Bierce, The Devil's Dictionary

255. Philosophy n. a favorite scam of those altogether incapable of earning an honest living; treatises written by those with a love for saying in many words what would be better off said in none

256. Psychiatry n. a discipline, masquerading as a science, populated by practitioners, posing as doctors, to treat disorders, highly lucrative

257. Psychologist n. a wannabe psychiatrist distinguished only from the philosopher by the possession of a richer clientele

258. Priest n. one who foists homilies on a sleeping congregation who later claim to have received spiritual sustenance

259. Bishop n. another homilist, like the priest except in his greater power to induce somnolence and praise for spiritual nourishment

260. Professor n. one adept at closing the minds of his students but too highly esteemed to get reprimanded; one who expounds theories which he doesn't quite grasp to students too sleepy to notice

261. Juror n. one who, with foggy vision, porous memory and ample prejudice, decides the fate of the accused

262. Good Lawyer phr. one who ably exploits the fine traits of the juror

263. Judge n. one who, having no clients to bilk, envies the lawyers, especially the good ones

264. Poets n. writers, the best of whom pen bad philosophy and the rest of whom deserve a turn in a pillory

265. Mountebank n. a charlatan who takes your money to his bank

266.Intellectual n. one whose intellect is squandered on the inconsequential; see, 'professor'

267. Prostitute n. one who, often with much to give, gives the wrong thing

268. Fortune Teller phr. one whose good fortune relies on the naivete of her clients; a fortunate phony

269. Undertaker n. one who, with grave demeanor and unctuous gestures, undertakes to relieve you of your funds

270. Grave Robber phr. an honest thief bent on destroying the fine trappings of the undertaker

271. Beggar n. one who, being either shameless or courageous, endures either the censure or praise of the fortunate

272.Diplomat n. one who, undeterred by contradictions, seeks to promote the amity of nations

273. Astrologer n. one who concocts lucrative scams by appealing to the positions of the unheavenly bodies

274. Police Officer phr. a minor government official too often vilified by the self-righteous and too often trusted by those too enamored of the State

275. Penny Stock Broker phr. one who peddles shares in companies soon to be defunct to clients soon to be broke

Vanity and Human Nature

The virtues lose themselves in self-interest like rivers in the sea.
François duc de La Rouchefoucauld Maxims

276. Human Nature phr. Nature having a bad day

277. Altruist n. one given to ostentatious displays of helping others in the hope that the
favors thus bestowed will be repaid tenfold

278. Egoist n. one who differs from the altruist only in his more devious ways of gaining an
advantage

279. The existence of altruism is more apparent in the animal kingdom than in genteel
society.

280. Our vanity reveals to others those of our flaws which we hide from ourselves.

281. We often decry the vanity of others and, in so doing, unwittingly proclaim our own.

282. Vanity n. a predisposition to impress others while making of oneself a fool

283. Vanity, unlike the body, defies the ravages of time.

284. Our vanity is a faithful friend in the face of betrayal by others.

285. The infallibility of our vanity denies us any desire for self-enlightenment.

286. Action n. the result of a motive, either disingenuous or misunderstood by the actor, usually both

287. Motive n. that which we poorly understand in regard to ourselves but have no trouble divining in others

288. One receives compliments according to how one perceives oneself.

289. Compliments are confirmations of one's self-esteem, both high and low.

290. Cynicism n. a view adopted after much careful observation of humanity only to be jettisoned as the mind grows feeble or strengthened as it grows sharper

291. Optimist n. one who, after having being forced to drink the dregs of the glass, considers it to be half full.

292. Pessimist n. a close cousin of the cynic who drinks only the fine wine at the top of the glass, having already anticipated the dregs at the bottom

293. Realist n. the favorite child of the pessimist and the cynic; one too modest to boast of his illustrious lineage

294. Know Thyself: an imperative leading to an assessment rejected in horror

295. To Thine Own Self Be True: a corollary of the preceding but perhaps more frightening

296. Schadenfreude n. what one experiences when one has no joy of one's own

297. Misanthrope n. one who, having witnessed the best in humanity, seeks a cave

298. Eremite n. a religious hermit summarily ejected from the cave by the misanthrope

299. The flaws of others are seen through the clouded lens of our vanity; but our most heinous flaws we see suspect not at all.

300. Those who take themselves too seriously are those with the best claim to be ignored.

.

301. Self-Righteous phr. adept at offloading one's sins onto others

Chance, Luck and Probability

Probability is the very guide to life. Bishop Joseph Butler

274. Chance n. a type of deceit responsible for enriching the house and bankrupting the poor; the world as a casino

275. Luck n. a high class whore available to the highest bidder, the rich–or so say the poor

276. Blessed adj. favored by chance or God, the distinction between the two being impossible to distinguish and of no material difference to those so favored

277. Bad Luck phr. out of favor with one's friends, family and relatives

278. Good Luck phr. see preceding

279. We consider some outcomes so terrible that we are prone to overestimate their risk at the expense of underestimating the danger of other possibilities more horrible and insidious.

280. Probability n a simple and reliable calculus for happiness offered to all but with few takers; that which gives the lie to luck and chance

281. Risk n. that which is either too readily run or too frequently avoided based on too little evidence

The Rich And The Poor

281. Debtor's Prison phr. an archaic hellhole domiciling those with the bad judgment to be poor; in nowise different than its contemporary scion

282. Less is more or so the rich tell the poor, the latter being too susceptible to such silly lore.

283. Waste Not Want Not: a proverb wasted on the rich and an insult to the poor

284. Windfall n. the gold filled ship of the poor forever moored in the harborharbor.

Virtues

The virtuous man contents himself with dreaming that
which the wicked man does in real life.
Sigmund Freud, "The Interpretation of Dreams"

284. Tolerance n. the attitude one demands of others in order to do as one wishes

285. Compassion n. what we liberally give to others when their sorrows demand little of our time; the virtue which, when sincerely rendered, does more good in the world than any other

286. Patience n. a cardinal virtue urged by the rich upon the poor

287. Charity n. that given to the poor with no material loss to the giver; a donation expecting a plaudit

288. Honesty n. an objective appraisal of others best kept to oneself or shared with the enemies of the one so assessed

289. Forgiveness n. that which is easy to give after revenge has been exacted

290. Good adj. a property one assigns to someone based upon their willingness to be one's sycophant; a class including most dogs and husbands: 'fetch good dog', 'fetch good husband'

291. Constancy of Regret phr. the accurate measure of the insincerity of one's apologies

292. Civility n. that which, like friendship, is lost in a dispute over the trivial

293. Courage n. fortitude in the face of a toothless enemy; that from which one shies when no one is watching

294. Coward n. one with the extraordinary ability to distinguish prudence from folly

295. Hero n. a coward with just enough strength to exploit a lucky opportunity

296. Compassion and cynicism may co-exist in the wisest of souls, and usually do.

297. Humility n. the humble acknowledgement that one knows a fair amount about about a few things, a little about more things and nothing about most things

298. Modesty n. a desire to redirect the conversation to one's own accomplishments after having seen it turned to another's

299. Kindness and compassion are kindred spirits, as are cynicism and understanding.

300. Inquisitiveness n. a propensity incurring the disfavor of the world and the ire of one's teacher

301. Remorse n. a spurious display of feeling calculated to spare oneself the revenge of the injured or a premature trip to the gallows, the two being equally gruesome

Doubt, Belief, and Truth

*If you be a real seeker after the truth, it is necessary that you doubt at
Least once in your life, as far as possible, all things.
Rene Descartes, The Principles of Philosophy*

302. Skeptic n. one who professes to know nothing while laboring to prove that know one knows anything

303. Enlightenment n. a tear in the veil of ignorance, such tears being most frequently proclaimed by those with the most intact veils

304. If you wish to know the truth, look first for evidence which would falsify your view; and if you find it, which you certainly will, get a new view.

305. The surest way to prove oneself wrong is to start with the intransigent belief that one is right.

306. Belief n. a condition of myopia afflicting both its votaries and detractors; a stumbling block on the road to the truth

307. Conviction n. a type of belief seldom encountered when limited to that which is thoroughly understood

308. Truth n. that which is claimed by the many, questioned by the few and never espoused by the wise

309. One readily believes without evidence that which one desires most.

310. View n. that which is stubbornly clung to by its proponents in the face of contravening evidence

311. Evidence n. that which changes by the minute but which is cited by those who believe it immutable

312. Open Mind phr. the type of mind found only in essays written by those oblivious to reality; see 'optimist'

313. How n. a question asked when we don't understand why

314. Point Of View phr. a vantage point from which one's views become progressively narrower

315. Doubt n. the final destination of those who have arduously sought the Truth

316. Most people believe many more truths than me because they believe much more than me.

317. Be careful lest you exchange small truths for dangerous falsehoods.

318. Cherish the finest of your beliefs for they are likely few and come at a great cost.

319. Certainty n. a state of mind succeeding a blow on the head with a cudgel

320. Doubt, properly understood, accomplishes what certainty never can.

321. To ask the unanswerable is a fool's game politely declined by the wise.

322. What I once thought that I knew, I now believe to be absurd; and much of what I now think that I know will doubtless befall the same fate. The truth stays a step ahead of belief.

323. De Omnibus Dubitandum: Doubt everything–more Latin wisdom applicable to those who would grow wise through error; attributed to many thinkers, both religious and secular

Modern Monstrosities

324. Social Media phr. a vast wasteland littered with the assertions of the irrational in the hope of convincing the unreasonable; a cogent refutation of the principle of freedom of speech

325. Internet News phr. a digital vacuum befouled by the pompous writings of those who fancy it their duty to disabuse the world of its misguided ways, the world being quite willing to oblige; pablum for those allergic to a more nourishing diet

326. Fact-Checker phr. an execrable creature of recent origin who arbitrates the truth with his own facts

327. Facebook n. a platform where posters, mostly self-absorbed, display information, usually trivial, to an audience, rarely interested; digitized egoism

328. Politically Incorrect phr. the censure one heaps upon others who speak the truth about the latest posturings of the morally sanctimonious; the authoritarian attempt to control language and thought

Love and the Heart

The Heart Has Reasons Which Reason Cannot Understand.
Blaise Pascal, Pensées

329. Love n. A state of nervous excitation confused with infatuation to which it bears little resemblance; an indefinable notion occupying poets to unhealthy extent; an inflammation of the heart, its diagnosis being the function of the bilious liver

330. The allure of passionate love, much like a siren, never delivers what it promised but always, for better or worse, brings more than expected.

331. Heart n. the subject of a thousand happy metaphors, none of them agreeable to the other organs

332. In affairs of reason, fear and and its absence are largely driven by our assessment of risk. In matters of the heart, risk plays no role.

333. Fear n. a dagger which strikes at the heart and is never fully removed, its pernicious effects lingering forever

334. There is no better clue to one's heart than one's treatment of animals.

335. To lead one's life according to the heart is to court disappointment and peril but not to do so is not to live.

336. Profound or sentimental–it matters not unless it moves the heart.

337. Fire n. the future embers of a passionate heart

338. Where the heart is concerned, the suffering of one touches all.

339. A hardened heart foregoes all that is worthwhile.

340. Question all but the voice of the heart.

341. Love found in the ugliest of places is beauty revealed.

342. Love unexpressed may lie hidden in the hearts of the timid.

343. Lonely is the heart which loves the most.

344. Unrequited Love phr. a blessing in disguise

345. Lose the love of your life and darkness descends, but the fire of light is heaven sent.

346. Omnia Vincit Amor: Love conquers all–an expression meaning either 'Love makes a slave of all' or 'All of one's troubles are overcome by love'--both interpretations attesting to the weakness and dependency of loves subjects

347. Reflections about passionate love are mostly ignored by the young and come too late for the old.

348. Both falling in and out of love are matters over which we have no say.

349. Love, by a swift legerdemain, leads us blithely into suffering.

350. To conquer suffering, submit first to love.

351. Love comes uninvited and departs unnoticed.

352. Love, curiously enough, is seldom a bete noire to those having suffered its deceit.

353. Love would be our most beloved teacher if not for the opacity of its many masks.

354. Love for the idea of love persists when love does not.

355. Love accompanied by vanity dies soon.

354. Love jugulates lovers as does a lion a gazelle.

355. From love to the well too often, from love to hell too soon…

356. Nostalgia for long lost loves never dies and returns when we least expect it.

357. Love is oblivious to all but the present.

358. Morality confronts romantic love in a battle which both are destined to lose.

359. What moves the heart moves the soul which, in its turn, moves the world.

Animals

Until one has loved an animal, a part of one's soul remains unawakened.
Anatole France

360. Baby n. a ruddy and wrinkled blob occasioning much lying and insincere flattery, such fulsome displays being heartily approved by the parents; a creature to which the enhanced cuteness of kittens is attributable

361. We would all do well to emulate the candor of animal communication.

362. Cat n. a clever animal chiefly remarkable for its uncanny ability to reduce its owner to a life of servitude

363. Dog n. an animal who, through much drooling and fawning, achieves the same result as the cat

364. Pig n. a highly intelligent beast lacking the vocal capacity to dissuade its executioner; in nowise a member of God's elect

365. Cow n. another cognitively advanced animal immensely larger than the pig but afflicted with the same vocal insufficiency and destined for the same fate; like the pig in failing to make the cut

366. Lemming n. a herd follower indistinguishable from most humans in its inability to steer clear of dangerous cliffs

367. Sheep n. a stolid, herd follower like the lemming and the human except in its aversion to the precipice

368. Bird n. a winged marvel free from earthly shackles, frequently devoured by its raptorial brethren

369. Cicada n. a lowly wight provoking much wonder by chirruping every seventeenth year; one of God's most annoying creatures

370. Cricket n. an annoying little fellow tirelessly playing a strident solo on a starry night; another of God's unaccomplished musicians but a persistent on nonetheless

371. Frog n. a slimy amphibian whose croaks herald the advent of spring and a joyous redivivus; God with laryngitis

372. Fox n. a beautiful animal, revered for its slyness and pelt, hunted by those praised for their choice of weapons

373   Snake n. a beneficial creature much maligned for a trait, deceitfulness, which it does not possess

374. Shrew n. a bloodthirsty member of the soricidae family, or a harridan of no particular tribal affiliation

375. Spider n. A fearsome creature who, like the wife, eviscerates her mate

376. Snake in the Grass phr. one adept at hiding deadly intentions; another unjust vilification of an innocent creature

377. Every stray cat should have a name.

378. Venomous Snake phr. a legless reptile, usually timid, feared by humans, usually ignorant; the fear of the unknown exposed

379. Lion n. a lazy feline much venerated for its predilection for sleep, food and sex, such appetites being satisfied by its harem

380. Lioness n. a ferocious huntress and champion of antifeminism

381. Angels come most often in the guise of stray cats, and so they go unrecognized.

382. We would pamper toads and frogs were it not for our perceived cuteness of kittens.

383. Cats intuit grief to a degree which humans never attain, though both are equally selfish.

384. Porcupine n. a clumsy mammal covered with sharp dorsal quills to deter predators, its vulnerable underbelly lacking such equipage

385. Black Mamba n. a venomous snake widely considered by ophidiologists to be the deadliest creature on God's earth, such scientists being happily oblivious to another animal, the human

Liars and Lies

No man has a good enough memory to be a successful liar.
Abraham Lincoln

386. Lie n. that which, given our instinct for self-preservation, comes more easily than the truth.

387. Hypocrite n. one aware of the prudence of endorsing all sides of an issue; one who adopts the "Do as I say, not as I do" philosophy in order to do as one wishes without censure

388. Loyal adj. having yet to see any advantage in switching to the other side

389. We often have more to learn from those who speak falsely than we do from those who speak the truth.

390. Liar n. one finally convinced of the inexpediency of telling the truth

Law and Punishment

Lawyers are the only persons in whom ignorance of the law is not punished.
Jeremy Bentham, Notebook with Unique Golden Marble Touch

391. Eyewitness n. one who, with blurred vision, porous memory and ample prejudice decides the fate of the accused

392. Innocent Until Proven Guilty phr. the essence of a legal maxim designed, in theory, to protect the rights of the accused; but, in practice, its contrary being more commonly applied, ensures his conviction

393. De Minimis Non Curat Lex: The law does not care about small matters–an apparent open invitation to petty criminals to commit minor offenses, the law having precisely the opposite in mind, attending harshly to small transgressions while winking at the large

394. Law n. a farrago of unintelligible principles exploited by lawyers for personal gain and, secondarily, for the conviction of their clients

395. Ganch v. to execute a criminal by dropping him onto sharp iron stakes to deter future offenders from being on the wrong side of justice and the powerful

396. Bastinado v. a to punish, in Draconian manner, by lacerating the soles of the feet by blows administered with a switch, such manner of retribution being more feared by the miscreant than a quick ganching

397. Decollate v. to remove the head of a criminal thereby rendering his brain incapable of plotting future mischief; a judicious use of the guillotine

398. Hanging n. a form of punishment similar to decollation except that it is more likely to go awry, leaving the hanged one another happy moment to repent his sins

Science

*Great is the power of steady misrepresentation—but the history of science shows
how, fortunately, this power does not endure long.*
Charles Darwin, On the Origin of Species

399. Science n. an enterprise for establishing certain kinds of truths,
usually cited by those with no knowledge of it history or methodology

400. Taxonomy n. a pig-headed attempt to pigeonhole Nature

401. Long Range Forecast phr. a prediction, almost always false, made
to support a view, patently absurd, to invigorate its adherents, forever
clueless

402. Hermeneutics n. the science which encourages a thousand
misinterpretations

403. Science brings knowledge, and knowledge of the limits of science
brings enlightenment.

404. Creationism n. a tall tale told by preachers, long on greed, to their
flocks, short on brains

405. Explain Scientifically phr. to relegate the marvelous to the mundane

406. Science without skepticism is superstition.

Advice

The old are fond of giving good advice; it consoles them for no longer being able to set a bad example.
François de la Rochefoucauld, Maxims

The only thing to do with good advice is pass it on; it is never of any use to oneself.
Oscar Wilde

407.

408. Know Thyself: an ancient saw best ignored if one wishes to live happily

409. To Thine Ownself Be True: a corollary of the preceding urging the behavior of either a monster or a saint, neither being less objectionable than the other

410. Play No Favorites: an imperative which, if heeded, ensures the making of many enemies; an admonishment to skewer everyone equally

411. Advice n. that which one liberally bestows upon others in the vain hope that the favor will go unreciprocated

412. Good Advice phr. that which everyone claims to want while avoiding it like the plague.

413. Think For Yourself: more dubious advice which, by the grace of the Heavens, is rarely followed; but when taken leads to flagellation or worse

413. Think For Yourself: more dubious advice, which, by the grace of the Heavens, is rarely followed; but when taken leads to flagellation or worse.

The Young and the Old

Youth is wasted on the young. George Bernard Shaw.

414. We were all once misled, and never more insidiously so, by the passions of youth.

415. The experience of age may be a great thing if it loses not the passion of youth.

416. The young think they are immortal, and the old cannot forgive God for ever having been young.

417. Old Age phr. a time for casting off those fears which inhibited us in youth, leaving us free to commit those actions of which we are no longer capable

418. The habits of youth are the regrets of old age or its fondest memories, the two sentiments often coexisting

419. Old age is the triumph of the intellect over the passion of youth, such victory being a Pyrrhic one.

420. Mortality n. a rarely considered abstraction for the young and a companion specter for the old

421. Old Age phr. Nature's last laugh at the expense of the young

422. Old age is the tragedy of fulfilled youth.

Nature

423. Nature n. a mighty force created by the Almighty to inspire poets and raze villages.

424. Nature sings and is then silent, but Nature's songs and silence have much to say to those who will listen.

425. The song of the thrush surpasses the collective wisdom of the greatest philosophers.

426. Fall Flowers phr. the last stand of the fragile against the inexorable march of Nature

427. Powerless adj. subjected to the fury of Nature or the wrath of one's spouse, the latter being the more terrifying

428. One chorus of Nature is silenced by another and that by another until one finally listens.

Drunkenness

Work is the curse of the drinking classes. Oscar Wilde

429. Drunkard n. one who swaps one type of incarceration for another, wisdom for regret

430. Drunkenness delivers great insights; headaches and hebetude douse them with reality.

431. Drunkenness puts on rose colored glasses; hangovers shatter them.

432. Booze n. A divine elixir which, unlike reason, distinguishes us from the higher animals

433. Sober adj. a myopic state curable by beer

434. In Vino Veritas: In wine there is truth–an insight attributed to Pliny the Elder meaning either wine enables one to see the truth or wine reveals the truth about the speaker by loosening his tongue, probably both

Imagery

427. The innocent die before God in the icey vastness of emerald silence.

428. There is nothing so delightful as the nighttime whistle of a train roaring over a distant plain.

429. The night time susurrus of the wind through trees is the most powerful antidote for anxiety.

430. Fireflies on summer nights compose paeans to God.

431. From the penetralia of my mind arise the thoughts which perplex and disturb me most, the darkest of which I would fain believe are not my own.

432. Our loves and passions unfold beneath the light of a logical sun and fade away in the
still-wind chambers of our hearts.

433. Motionless gray clouds in a black sky pierced by a lone star give reasons for God unseen by those with their nose to the ground.

434. Tall white flowers cloaked in darkness bend toward the coming light of dawn.

435. Haunting is the cry of the screech owl in foggy woods at night.

436. Solitude n. sitting alone at night, thought suspended, engulfed by the vastness of Nature

437. Fog n. A ghostly veil engulfing mountains, vales and marshes; Nature inviting one to observe closely

438. Vast depths impenetrable by light house fantastical chimera as mysterious as heaven's stars.

439. We all die alone, specks on a dark shore, cloaked by unforgiving black clouds.

440. Melting Stars phr. soft lights diffused through dark clouds seen as formless ghosts in the Heavens.

441. November crickets on a cold night sing Nature's elegy to death.

442. Fall Flowers phr. the last stand of the fragile against the inexorable march of Nature.

443. Dance–dance merrily–on the black gallows of Mortality.

444. The light which burns away suffering can only be seen through the darkness.

445. Storms in the night bring languorous contemplation to those ensconced in comfortable beds and naked terror to those who wander dark corridors.

446. The pitiable die in a dark vacuum surrounded by those too careworn to mourn their passing.

447. Massive black demons oversee fiery rivers engulfing those who long for Hell.

448. The dawn breaks and the terrors of the damned recede if but for a moment.

449. Sad white doves fly beneath a leaden sky and above crumbling churches bereft of love.

450. Skeletons, blanched and chilled, clatter menacingly through a mountain cemetery.

451. Lost are the loves of the heart, lost forever in a strange prison on the edge of the universe

452. The silent blackness of night caresses the heart, revives the soul and terrifies the mind.

453. Fall moths flutter away from the light and into the misty obscurity of winter.

454. Dance on the graves of angels and demons if you dare.

455. Through a hazy, orange brume the wayfarer will essay the long journey home.

456. On a starlit plain swirling with bats, a coven of witches offer human sacrifices to their hircine master.

457. The shrieks of the mad caged in glass houses are heard, if at all, only by God.

458. The beauty of the day fades into misty Eternity and returns in the gilded light of dawn.

459. What music cannot inspire is dead to the world.

Enlightenment

454. Enlightenment n. a tear in the veil of ignorance, such tears being most frequently proclaimed by those with the most intact veils

455. Epiphany n. a sudden, supposedly life-altering revelation in which the life altered soon returns to its prior state of ignorance; the unexpected awareness that one's past has been a sham and that the future will be no better

456. Empathizing v. feeling the feeling of another, such shared feeling resulting in either compassion or abhorrence

457. Mad adj. characterizing a state of perspicacity unknowable to rational minds

458. Maladjusted adj. enlightened

459. There is nothing more humbling or enlightening than to discover that one is not as perceptive as one had thought, the rare occurrence of such discoveries being the principal reason for the scarcity of the aforementioned awakenings.

460. Ignorance is bliss except in its longevity.

Logic

Logic is invincible, because in order to combat logic it is necessary to use logic.
Pierre Boutroux

Logic n. the art of thinking and reasoning in strict accordance with the limits
and incapacities of the human misunderstanding
Ambrose Bierce, The Devil's Dictionary

460. Logic n. an enterprise employed by those foolish enough to venture to convince the unreasonable; the art of intellectual self-defense; a pariah in an irrational world

461. Reason can accomplish much of importance once it acknowledges that there is much of
importance which it cannot know.

462. Argument n. a foolish dispute where the winner makes an enemy

463. Foregone Conclusion phr. a conclusion which should never have been drawn before; one which the wise always forgo

464. Paradox n. a puzzling contradiction meant to vex mathematicians and logicians who, having already wasted too much of their time in discovering it, waste more in an attempt to solve it.

465. Hasty Generalization phr. a rush first to judgment and then to prejudice

466. Expert n. one lauded by the masses for delivering false predictions ex cathedra

467. Irrational Thinking phr. a type of thinking usually presenting in the seductive guise of
 its contrary and having the uncanny ability to mislead an otherwise intelligent majority

467. Rationality n. a faculty feared in others by those with an agenda

468. Non Sequitur phr. Latin for 'does not follow'--the type of argument which most are disposed to follow

469. Ad Misericordiam phr. A type of logical fallacy which eschews evidence and appeals
 to the sympathy of its audience, thereby recruiting a legion of sentimental lunk-heads

470. Petitio Principii adj. a type of circular reasoning in which the arguer petitions the listener to accept a conclusion on the presupposition that it is already true; the successful cramming of a square head into a round hole

471. Logical Fallacy phr. a bit of reasoning which most find quite logical and most palatable to their partis pris

472. Reason n. a vestigial trait possessed by humans, its full blown embodiment doubtless having been present in an extinct species as yet undiscovered

473. Ad Baculum phr. a type of paralogism which substitutes the cudgel for reason, such succedaneum being especially effective when aimed at the brains of the fearful

474. Ad Populum phr. a specious species of argument appealing to the opinion of the majority, not unsurprisingly persuasive to those who count themselves members of aforementioned class

475. Ad Verecundiam phr. one of divers fallacies depending for it success on the unquestioned reverence for a questionable authority

476. Ad Hominem phr. referencing the bad character of one's opponent in the hope that the bad judgment of one's audience will suffice as a refutation of said adversary

Friends and Enemies

Always forgive your enemies; nothing annoys them so much. Oscar Wilde

478. True friendship is unlike fine wine in that, while both are rare and scintillate with age, the former need not be consumed to be enjoyed.

479. Loneliness n. a feeling more common in the company of true friends than false ones

480. Silence n. the most powerful form of communication between true friends

481. Civility n. that which, like friendship, is lost in a dispute over the trivial

482. Rich adj. having many friends and a bulging purse, the loss of the latter decimating the number of the former

483. Enemy n. a quondam friend having achieved great success or a current one quietly bent on destroying yours

484. Acquaintances outlast friendships, because the former require no work.

485. I love all my friends and hate all my enemies. Now, if only I had the discernment to tell them apart…

485. I love all my friends and hate all my enemies. Now, if only I had the discernment to tell them apart…

Beauty

Beauty, true beauty, ends where intellectual expression begins. Oscar Wilde

485. Beauty n. a quality proclaimed by those, not favored with its possession, to be only skin deep

486. Homely adj. describing one with an unappreciated je ne sais quoi; beauty wasted on
 blind

487. Comely adj. the opposite of homely, the two being interchangeable depending on time, convention and the fickle taste of the beholder

488. Amaranth n. an imaginary flower reputed by those with beautiful souls to possess everlasting beauty

Dreams and Nightmares

489. Dream n. a parade of phantasmagorical images revealing to the dreamer a bizarre recreation of a long forgotten but still important past; a night time provoker of nostalgia

490. Sleep n. an escape from the demons of the day into the nightmares of the void

491. Nightmare n. a legion of terrifying ghouls unleashed from our subconscious when we are most at their mercy

492. Sleep is the lethe which seldom comes to troubled minds.

Education

I never let my schooling interfere with my education. Mark Twain

Education is an admirable thing, but it is well to remember that nothing that is worth knowing can be taught. Oscar Wilde

493. Educated adj. having acquired an uninquisitive mind at great parental or societal expense

494. Erudite adj. having surpassed the merely educated in the acquisition of facts and in the ossification of the mind

495. University n. an exalted institution where wide-eyed matriculants come for a sound dose of indoctrination and leave pronouncing themselves the saviors of the world

496. Autodidact n. a self-taught person having escaped the stultification of a formal education and a lifetime burden of debt

497. Inquisitiveness n. a propensity incurring the disfavor of the world and the ire of one's teacher

Mind

Fortune favors the prepared mind.
Louis Pasteur

498. Mind n. a ghostly substance, presumably domiciled in the head, with a mysterious talent for solving the even more mysterious riddles of life; a master charlatan

499. The mind is shoddy equipment indeed for unraveling the mystery of existence.

500. The mind persistently and annoyingly asks questions which it cannot answer.

501. The malleability of the mind is a boon for those who would mold it to evil purpose.

Miscellaneous

502. Sage n. a hoary gentleman renowned for the inanity of his pronouncements

503. We often lose hold of things rare and priceless in the quest for things slight and ephemeral.

504. Indifference n. a state succeeding passion and signaling that all is lost

505. Original adj. having been said time and again and which, if said yet again, only bores once again

506. Genius n. one admired by the many for influential works misexplained by the few

507. Imagination n. that which promises relief from the tedium and brutality of the world while increasing our vulnerability to both

508. Hatred n. a visceral feeling which, as if it were an acid, eats away at the insides of its possessor but does little harm to its object

509. Dreamers n. those whose aspirations usually exceed their grasp and whose passion inspires others to the same folly

510. War n. God's provision for worms, undertakers and priests

511. Cemetery n. a plot of land where the dead sleep well if not disturbed by memorials offered by the living

512. Hypocrite n. one who adopts the "do as I say not as I do" philosophy in order to do as one wishes without censure; one wishing to keep the important vices for oneself

513. Compliment n. that which the receiver is unlikely to believe if not already convinced of its truth; that which the receiver acknowledges as confirming the superior acumen of the giver; that which, when given too frequently, defeats its purpose: to curry favor with another

514. Condescending adj. characterizing an action intended to intimidate one's superior

515. Goal n. a siren song for those too hard headed to have learned from disappointment

516. Striving v. headed for disappointment

517. Failure n. that seen in retrospect to have been a blessing; a misguided goal unaccomplished

518. Silence n. the mantra of those who learn little from listening and nothing from speaking

519. Silent! interj. an injunction offered to suppress the loquacity of a speaker for the mercy of a captive audience

520. Quiet adj. having the decency not to afflict others with tinnitus

521. Rainbow n. a brilliant, arced spectrum of color at the end of which lies either a pot of gold if you're rich or a kettle of dross if you ain't.

522. Ghost n. a wispy spirit who, having nothing better to do, haunts the living; a phantom misspending its afterlife

523. Reaping What One Sows phr. good or bad karma depending on one's intentions or the caprices of Nature

524. Insult n. a barb launched at the superior accomplishments of another

525. Powerless adj. subjected to the fury of Nature or the wrath of one's spouse, the latter being the more terrifying

526. Ideals n. vain hopes forever shifting in accord with one's age and material position in life; what one has when one has no money or too much of it.

527. Thick-Skinned phr. indifferent to the petty slights and envious snipings of others; that is, generally indifferent

528. Well-Adjusted phr. having been diagnosed with at least one of the spurious disorders of psychiatry–the more such diagnosed disorders the better adjusted

529. Delusional adj. having a firm grasp of reality misdiagnosed as an abnormality by those who grasp it the least; see 'well-adjusted'

530. The light at the end of a dark tunnel is too often the beacon toward a darker one.

531. A cynic's best friend is his dog, one with big fangs and an ill-temper.

532.Old Wives Tale phr. a type of tale more likely told by pseudoscientists and old husbands than their wives

533. Heaven Forbid! an exclamation expressing the desire that something terrible not happen when it already has or almost certainly will

534. Good For Nothing phr. a description of one presumably once good for something but whose current condition permits no further exploitation

535. Hypocrite n. one keenly attuned to the benefits of endorsing all sides of an issue; one who adopts the "Do as I say, not as I do" philosophy in order to do as one wishes without censure; one wishing to keep the important vices for oneself

536. Effrontery n. the audacity to speak the truth about another rather than to tactfully keep one's mouth shut; the best way to lose a false friend

537. Wilderness n. a vast and beautiful tract of land soon to succumb to the saw and the bulldozer

538. Hedonist n. one who, seeking a life of pleasure, travels the primrose path only to find it bare of flowers, most notably primroses

539. The Devil May Care phr. having at least one friend

540. Shadow n. a silhouette having at least as much substance as its caster

541. Stray n. a lost soul ignored by all except the kind and the eccentric

542. Myth n. the mythologist's imagination unleashed upon Nature, the favor being returned by Nature to Her detractor

543. Mythologist n. one who transfers the fearsome traits of Nature into the misdeeds of of the gods

544. The views of others may seem preposterous. Be kind. It may be all they have to misguide them through the treacherous shoals of life

545. Forever Lost phr. that which, to the sorrow of the living, recedes forever into oblivion

546. A net indiscriminately cast catches more offal than fish.

547. Beholden v. having acquired a formidable enemy; forever held in bondage

548. Weltanschauung n. a comprehensive view of the world fashioned from fragmentary observations and a smidgen of knowledge; a welter of contradictions unrecognized by the holder of such

549. Half-Wit phr. having twice as much wit as most others, the quarter-wits

550. Storms in the night bring languorous contemplation to those ensconced in comfortable beds and naked terror to those who wander dark corridors.

551. There are those who cannot be happy unless they fancy themselves offended by another, such other being in every way superior to the offended.

552. Those who take themselves too seriously are the ones with the best claim to be ignored.

553. Advertisement n. a clever attempt to create an artificial want in an audience eager to accept it.

554. Fire n. the future embers of a passionate heart

555. Loneliness n. cruelty inflicted by longevity

556. Those who keep company with the lost will dance with angels

557. A sentiment of Draconian retribution for one who does a cruelty to the innocent is neither ignoble nor immoral; it is the lack of such sentiment which is to be decried.

558. Shallow minds sometimes get it right; great minds seldom do. Therein lies the paradox of thought

559. The pitiable die in a dark vacuum surrounded by those too careworn to mourn their passing.

560. Surrealism n. a brilliant transmogrification of the unreal into the fantastic

561. The theories of great minds are priceless though rarely true.

562. A trillion stars shining brightly and the brilliance of God shed no light on the suffering of humanity and animals.

563. Cynicism, compassion and the heart forge the path toward wisdom

564. Grief displayed before the world is the most shameless form of egoism.

565. Suffering kept to oneself is the soul of bravery.

566. Suffer stoically those misfortunes which would crush you the most, suffer in that way lest you cause yourself great harm.

567. More Of The Same phr. too much of a bad thing

568. Closed Mind phr. a prison from which its inhabitants neither can nor want to escape; a cloister offering maximum comfort

569. Subjectivity n. the opposition of one's inner longings against the might of Reality, for the former a losing proposition

570. Vegetarianism n. a type of diet which promotes eupepsia, health and a reduction in the slaughter of higher animals

571. To endure one's greatest misfortune one is prone to invoke the supernatural or the theurgical, a feckless attempt given that both are unlikely to exist or at best not to care

572. De Gustibus Non Est Disputandum: a Latin principle meaning "There is no disputing about taste"--said principle being warmly embraced by those with bad taste, disputed by those with no taste and amusingly dismissed by those with good taste

573. Sarcasm n. a sharp tool for unmasking inanity and arrogance, a tool best wielded by those under attack from both

574. Intuition n. the "cognitive faculty" averred by the benighted to surpass all others as the diviner of the Truth; a fabrication more mysterious than what it is claimed to know

575. Hunch n. a type of intuition concerned with the prosaic rather than the sublime; the only member of its species with some claim to legitimacy

576. Ipsos Custodes? Who will keep watch over the guardians?--a question with the implicit answer, "another more able guardian and for that one yet another one still more able…"--an answer serving as a chilling warning to beware of one's protector, especially one's sovereign or state

577. Hysteria n. A child of the media having the terrifying ability to induce absurd beliefs and dangerous behaviors, two salient features not lost on politicians

578. Stoic n. one who foregoes the joys of life in favor of a faulty distinction between attitude and circumstance, the former being mostly determined by others and the latter being the instrument of our demise

579. An affinity for those ungrateful and indifferent is the result of spending too much time with them.

580. Ingratitude n. a condition resulting from a keen insight into what one's benefactor wishes to keep hidden

581. Idiocy attended by arrogance is repugnant; idiocy happily borne may charm us.

582. Defindit Numeris: There is safety in numbers–a bit of advice heeded by opportunistic politicians and their slavish minions

583. Damned v. condemned to Hell for God only knows what bad reason

584. Hunger n. that which gnaws at the stomach and indicts the world and God

585. Liberal n. the antithesis of the conservative, both being the antithesis of good will and reason

586. Culture n. the fictitious construct of do gooders intent upon reinventing it in their own image

587. All For Naught phr. not at all important in the first place

588. Absolutist n. one who affirms absolutely what absolutely cannot be known

589. Relativist n. one absolutely opposed to absolutism except in the defense of relativism or the rejection of one's relatives

590. Hedonist n. one who, seeking a life of sensual pleasure, travels the primrose path only to find it bare of flowers, most notably the primrose

590. Primrose Path phr. a path bare of primroses traveled by those bare of the will to seek a less seductive flower

590. Universe n. all that there is, spawned from that which which never was; see 'paradox'

591. Ex Nihilo Nihil Fit: Nothing is created from nothing; see 'universe'

592. I put more words in my cat's mouths than they have thoughts in their heads.

593. Someone who has no one drifts alone into death and, if the universe be kind, into Heaven

594. Mystic n. one whose studied silence hides either sagacity or stupidity, the answer to which being of no consequence, especially to the mystic

595. Hindsight Is Twenty Twenty: a proverb describing a type of sight with no more visual acuity than its predecessor, frontsight

596. Personality n. another fictitious construct invented by those with a love for ridiculing others with engaging characters

597. Bad Character phr. See 'personality'

598. Mugwump n. one who straddles the fence between two unreasonable views

599. Usurer n. one whose license to steal is valid only for the poor

Marriage

By all means, marry. If you get a good wife then you'll be happy.
If you get a bad one then you'll be a philosopher.
Socrates

Marriage is a wonderful institution, but who wants to live in an institution?
Groucho Marx

598. Marriage n. a holy union superior in every way to a heathen one, except in its brevity

❖ that which, in its contemporary manifestation, is quickly jettisoned when no longer novel

❖ a state of entwinement due to naivete, infatuation or a misguided sense of duty

❖ a peculiar custom soon to be archaic, or least so promised the ancients

599. Marriage Vows phr. a litany of fair warnings

600. Until Death Do You Part phr. one of the litany which too soon lapses into a wish for one's own demise

601. For Richer Or Poorer phr. a troth spoken by those expecting to become rich or those having never been poor

602. For Better Or Worse phr. a disjunction where the temporal order of the disjuncts determines the amount of happiness in the marriage: if better then small, and if worse then none at all

603. Polygamy n. multiple connubial ties undertaken by those with the good judgment to commit all of their indiscretions concurrently rather than in succession; see 'greed'

604. Monogamy n. a single conjugal knot promising boredom, aversion and infidelity, in no particular order; see 'envy'

Writing and Writers

We write to taste life twice, in the moment and in retrospect. Anais Nin

603. Novel n. the elaboration of a bad short story or the ruination of a good one

604. Conclusion n. the anxiously awaited end to a boring story or the false point implied by one

605. Poets n. writers, the best of whom pen bad poetry and the rest of whom pen bad philosophy

606. Parable n. a brief tale, hopefully amusing, with a moral, never original, conceived by an author, better off gardening

607. Fabulist n. one who writes childish tales to delight and frighten children, such tales being racist, traumatizing and insensitive, according to progressives; that is, to those having forgotten what it's like to be a child

608. Poem n. a piece of writing which should rhyme or perhaps it should not. In either case, it should move us to tears, terror or express the sublime. The one exception is amphigory which has a higher purpose, the elicitation of laughter.

609 Aphorist n. one who writes pithy sayings in lieu of being able to write great novels or in preference to writing bad ones

610. An aphorism should be taken with a grain of salt in the hope of finding a grain of truth.

611. Preface n a thoughtful warning to those wishing to avoid a lengthy and tedious exposition, or a blessing to those desiring a good night's sleep

612. Epilogue n. an all too common extension of a literary bludgeoning

613. Title n. the best part of the book if not too long

614. An author who prefaces his work with instructions on how to read it ensures its double misinterpretation.

615. Great Writing phr. that which is written in a year after many years of experience and reflection

****

616. Look inward, look deep and find the stranger who dwells within; for he propels you against your will.

617. The beauty of the day fades into misty Eternity and returns in the gilded light of dawn.

618. Stock Market phr. the the province of tears shed by those too impatient to have taken due stock

619. Buy Stocks When There Is Blood In The Streets: cruel counsel given by Baron Rothschild to those whose blood is already flowing there

620. One Picture Is Worth A Thousand Words: a proverb true only in the sense that nary a fanged word is necessary to discredit a bad picture, and one hundred thousand cannot capture a good one

621. Emotion n. a neurological excitation repressing reason

622. The moment is all that matters, but upon the moment it is impossible to dwell.

623. Grain Of Truth phr. that which, attached to a mountain of falsehoods, passes for universal verity.

624. The depth of our thoughts is no measure of their accuracy.

625. Whistling Past The Graveyard phr. underestimating the rapacity of worms

626. Knave n. one who relieves you of your goods for a good cause, his own; see 'socialist'

627. Listening v. attuned to multiple sources of misinformation

628. Longanimity n. patient endurance of misfortune found in good listeners and in those having read this book

629. Alchemy n. an unhappy metaphor for life's endeavors

630. Rationality n. a faculty abhorred in others by those with an agenda

631. Miser n. one who is as mingy with his feelings as he is with his money

632. Hated adj. having too often and for too long spoken the truth about prejudices held by others

633. Appearance Versus Reality phr. a philosophical distinction proposed by philosophers lacking the acumen to discern the difference

635. Tragic adj. blind to good fortune

636. Cherish your dreams lest they die unnoticed in the maelstrom of life's circumstances.

638. There awaits us in Heaven, but as likely in Hell,
a strange menagerie of those who on earth knew us well.
They will greet us with love, or perhaps recoil in dread,
but with which of the two, it cannot be said.

639. Defame v. to tarnish another's character with the truth

640. I love all my friends and hate all my enemies; now, if I only had the discernment to tell them apart...

641. There live among us those who are monstrous and strange and those whose beauty is rare and subtle. The trick, of course, is to tell them apart.

642. Turn prevailing opinion on its head and you will become wise, or at least not a fool.

Deep Drivel and Philosophical Piffle

It's a much cleverer thing to talk nonsense than to listen to it.
Oscar Wilde The Importance of Being Earnest

"Well, in our country," said Alice, "you'd generally get to somewhere else–if you ran very fast for such a long time as we've been doing." "A slow sort of country!" said the Queen. Now, here, you see, it takes all the running you can do, to keep in the same place. If you want to get somewhere else, you must run at least twice as fast as that!"
Lewis Carroll, Through the Looking Glass

643. The ways of Nature and Humanity are wondrous; but against such marvels, cynicism stands alone, dark and menacing.

644. The greatest sadness in life resides in the impossibility of reliving the best moments of our lives with the passion which they deserved.

645. To appear wise to others deluge them with cryptic utterances, then smugly shrug your shoulders and smile enigmatically when they ask you what they mean.

646. We do things for many a year and then move on to other things for a similar time and so on we go until the doing of these things comes to an end. But what is the meaning of this? The only answer is that they meant a great deal at the time. But what is the meaning of that?

647. Most people think on the surface. That is a good thing for them; for their world view rules and they are made happy.

648. A needle in a haystack,
　　it's not so hard to find;
　　so like the meaning of life,
　　if you have but world enough and time.

649. When you discover the meaning of life, don't tell me; or better yet, hide it from yourself.
 It might be worse than you expected.

650. We grasp the profound in an instant and lose it in a moment.

651. I know much less than I thought but much more than you think.
 And if I learn some more, I'll let you know—I think.

652. Februaries are dull and gloomy months.
　　Their skies are seldom blue.
　　But alas, dear Februaries,
　　I'll much too soon run out of you.

653. Beneath the surface of what sounds profound often resides only a platitude.

654. When you walk in another's shoes, make sure they're too big if you want to understand them.

655. A moment in time occurred in a flash.
　　It came in an instant; it left in a dash.
　　I asked the Heavens why it hadn't persisted.
　　I was given the answer that it never existed.

656. Laugh first at yourself and then at others; they'll love you if you do.

658. A well placed comma is a writer's best friend.

659. I want to be a great writer. I always set my goals quite low.

660. I once had a cat who didn't like me.
    He'd do anything just to spite me.
    He was surly, mean and frightful.
    But for all of that, you guessed it,
    He was really quite delightful.

661. What we wish to keep secret about ourselves defines us best.

662. My day went slowly.
    I wondered when it would pass.
    Then I realized how lucky I would be
    if the rest of my days took note
    and just as long would last.

663. Laugh heartily at yourself or everyone else will do it for you.

664. Someone once asked me why I wasted my time writing such drivel.
I asked them why they wasted their time reading it. They responded
that they liked me and it's not likely that anyone else, myself included,
would assume such an onerous task.

665. The seeking is often preferable to that which it seeks.
And when that is so, paradoxically, more seeking should be sought.
Though I'm not so sure, I'm sure you know,
So I'll give it some more thought.

666. A current memory is merely a misremembrance of a past memory, which didn't get it right in the first place.

667. 'Floccinaucinihilipilification' is my favorite word.
   I'm happy to announce it.
   Now I'd be quite proud
   if I could but half pronounce it.

668. Our sins should be atoned for.
   But when that's done,
   Let's have some fun.
   And commit one thousand more.

669. I live in a baronial estate.
   It is so very fine.
   It has no walls or boundaries.
   It's magical and sublime.
   It's larger than the universe,
   this lovely castle I call mind.

670. By Chance or Providence, it cannot be said; for the ways of life cannot be read.

671. Memory, you promise us great things.
   You dress up like a harlequin.
   But in the end, your mask peel off,
   You're seen to be a charlatan.

672. It's life's cruelest tribulations rather than abstract philosophy which challenge our world views for better or worse

673 If you want to lose a lot, dwell a lot upon what you've already lost.

674. We all stumble along a brambly path,
  call it life or what you will.
  It's thorns pierce hearts and dreams
  until Fate has had its fill.

675. Philosophy cloaked in nonsense is bearable but only in small doses.

676. If I think hard enough,
  the right word always comes to me,
  but swirled in a mix with wrong ones,
  which makes it hard to see.
  But if, luckily, I espy it,
  it's always stuck with glue,
  to one of the nasty wrong ones,
  and of no use to me or you.

678. I had a kitten with whom I was smitten.
  She grew up to be fat, and lazy at that.
  We'd chit and we'd chat.
  She'd sit in my lap.
  She wove me a hat.
  I wove her a mitten.
  The hat was too big, too small was the mitten.
  If you believe all of this, you'll believe anything written.

679. Politics n. a fertile field for weeds and briars, loved by politicians and other liars

680. Lexicographer n. one who defines words without understanding them

681. The distinction between reality and illusion is reasonably clear;
  but in reality, there's no difference, my dear.

682. Philosophy which is neither nonsensical nor clever should never be read. Never, never!

683. About so many things, there's good reason to complain.
 So please dispense with reason and spare yourself some pain.

684. I got drunk; a great insight came to me.
 But now it's lost; gee thanks, sobriety.

685. It takes a multitude of moments to make the illusion of Time but only a single moment to confirm it.

686. Philosophy gives nonsense a bad name.

687. Reality and illusion, it's a philosophical delusion.
 It comes with many headaches, curses and confusion.
 It's apt to make one think one's mind one is a lose'n.

688. Life ends in divers ways.
    Each one of them is Fate.
    But Fate is quite ill-tempered.
    It always makes us wait.
    So knowledge of our ending,
    it comes a tad too late.

689. Philosophy triumphs common sense; nonsense triumphs them both.

690. Too much has been said, too little of it true. So please talk little lest this describe you.

691. Memory would be neither friend nor foe but for the sensitivity of the soul.

692. The black tides of life,
     the howl of its winds
     are the scourge of all romance,
     even before it begins.

693. A romance never begun may be more poignant than one gone
forever.

694. Memory is form whose content is experience.

695. There are none so little impressed by wit as the witless.

696. The meaning of our dreams,
 it can't be figured out.
 But what is known about them
 is that to go without them
 makes sleep a bland affair,
 tedious and empty
 and more than I can bear.

697. All nonsense poetry,
     I assert without deception,
     is charming and insane
     and worthy of reflection.
     But now I must admit,
     this one's the one exception.

698. Free will is a theory, a fine one at that.
     But is it quite true, I queried my cat.
     She purred and she purred
     then flippantly said,
     "It just doesn't matter.

Now get out of my bed."
So I pondered some more.
I pondered quite late.
I wondered if it's all just a matter of fate.
Perhaps it's free will.
Maybe the latter.
Perhaps she was right.
It is of no matter.

699. Free will, preordination,
chance and fate—
These are all theories,
and fine ones I state.
But which one's quite true,
I queried my cat.
She purred and she purred
then flippantly said,
"It just doesn't matter.
Now get out of my bed."
So I pondered some more.
I pondered for sure
About all of these views,
from the first to the latter.
Then finally concluded,
I was mad as a hatter.

700. Philosophy, you see,
is all about reality.
Truth, metaphysics, epistemology—
About these subjects,
I thought long and hard.
Soon I was trapped
in a beastly canard.

I fought and I wrangled
to become disentangled,
But the harder I struggled
the more I felt strangled.
When my cat came along,
I desperately asked
just how she proposed
I get out of its grasp.
She mused for moment
before she retorted,
"You must use all your smarts.
You must use all your wit,
And run from this horror, lickety-split."
That's what she said.
That's what she exhorted.

701. I dreamt last night about the nature of Time.
My dream was nightmarish and rattled my mind.
I awoke next morning only to find
that the dream hadn't left me, hadn't left me behind.
I asked of this fiend, "What's the meaning of this?"
It said with a snarl.
It said with a hiss.
"Go ask your cat.
She's the only one who can help you with that."
So I rushed to my cat
Who I knew could divine
The substance of dreams and the nature of Time.
I asked her to help me
She replied with a rhyme.
"It's a silly question but if you insist,
I'll tell you the truth; I'll tell you this.
These things are no mystery.

They do not exist.
Now fetch me my dinner and make good time.
I want turkey and gravy and mulberry wine."

702. To my cat, I firmly asseverated,
    "Language is messy and much overrated.
    It's rife with ambiguity.
    It promotes discontinuity.
    With ferocity and purpose,
    it'll do so in perpetuity."
    "Hold on, not so fast" my captious
    Cat demurred.
    "That's the silliest thing, the stupidest thing,
    I think I've ever heard.
    If it's language you've forsaken,
    it's the wrong road that you have taken.
    You're much to blind to see
    that language would not work for us
    without much clarity.
    Such confusion that you claim
    is but a rarity,
    and your comprehension of his topic
    is wanting and myopic."
    "Whoa!" I exclaimed,
    I think you've proved my case;
    for my misunderstanding
    puts language in its place."
    "Now listen," said my friend.
    for I'll not say this again.
    It is not the fault of words.
    It's not the fault of clauses.
    It's not the fault of phrases
    nor of any ill-timed pauses.

The fault, it must be said,
lies squarely in your head."

703. My cat delivered to me,
this peculiar bit of philosophy:
"Those with little knowledge are sometimes quite wise,
and those with quite a lot of it,
may be dullards in disguise."
"That's positively puzzling," I sighed in disbelief.
"From this little sophistry,
I beseech you for relief."
She looked at me with a grin,
a wide grin and a smile.
"Certainly I will tell you,
but you must wait a while."
I became exasperated, increasingly agitated,
for though it was but seconds,
for too long I'd been frustrated.
"Oh well, oh very well, I'll tell you
and hope it will avail you,
much relief from your travail.
Mere knowledge, as I see it, is just utility.
Too often fraught with hubris and futility.
While wisdom is certainty,
dancing with humility.

704. In a grove, idyllic and umbrageous,
My cat claimed something,
atrocious and outrageous.
"Justice should be blind,
but in reality,
that's not what you will find.
Its scales are always tilted

towards those who deserve it least;

for morality, dare I say it, is such a ghastly beast.

There's but one way to make it fair,

Perhaps two that I'll admit.

The first is simply and amorally–

to get rid of it.

It's the second I advise.

Any other is unwise.

Please give the scale to me,

and I will tune it expertly.

So that it will always say,

when my interests are in play,

'Give to each and every one of them,

each and every day,

a very special status,

in a very special way.'"

When I recovered from my shock,

I told her what I thought.

"Why that's inanity, insanity,

the very height of vanity.

You've eviscerated justice

with all of your profanity."

"Wait now," growled my cat.

"I've had enough of that.

If you had the scale in hand,

You'd tune it just like me.

You're no different than I am,

except that in your actions,

where it is clearly writ,

you're pompous, self-righteous and a hypocrite."

Now I must declare,

I'm chastened to admit,

her points were all well taken.

And that's the truth of it.

705. All of these aphorisms are false, fortunately.

706. All of these aphorisms are false, especially this one.

PARABLES

The Ambiguity of God

1. An atheist met a theist. The atheist queried, "How can you believe such rubbish?" The theist responded by pointing out a majestic eagle soaring overhead. They went their separate ways, each lamenting the blindness of the other. Soon after, one of them was struck dead by lightning while attempting to save a drowning child. Upon finding this out, the other rethought his views.

Moral: God gives up no secrets.

The Professor and the Dope Fiend

2. A dope fiend met a Professor of Literature. "What do you do for a living?" asked the dope fiend. "I critique the writings of others," answered the professor." "And what about you?" "Nothing, I simply live," responded the dope fiend. They parted ways. The dope fiend was soon after killed in a knife fight. The professor resumed his tedious critiques.

Moral: Tedium is death disguised as life.

The Priest and the Worm

3. A small child once prayed over a dead worm, entreating God to take the poor creature to Heaven. A priest witnessed this and said to the child, "Your innocence and compassion is your salvation." The child, somewhat frightened by this, smashed the worm and scurried away. That Sunday the priest delivered a sermon on the first half of what he has seen.

Moral: Never mar a good homily with the whole truth.

The Depressed Man and the Empathetic Dog

4. A man, having lost the love of his life, attended a riotous out on his host's couch. He awakened next morning to find a large dog with a

basketball size head lying across his chest. The dog laid his head on the man's cheek. The man's sorrows were not assuaged, but his gratitude knew no bounds.

Moral: The kindness of animals is not lost on those who need it most.

The Happy Man's Torment

5. A man and a woman engaged in a philosophical conversation over a fine dinner. Said the woman, "Being as cynical as you are, I am puzzled how you take any pleasure in life." "On the contrary," responded the man. "I am quite happy in my cynicism and take great joy in most everything I do. Therefore, I am never bored. There is, though, one thing which bothers me. I know that death will soon bring all this happiness to an end, and this realization torments me immeasurably, constantly." The woman looked askance at the man and exclaimed, "Oh, piffle! These conditions–happiness and torment–are mortal enemies. This is just another of your silly paradoxes." The man replied, "Nothing could be further from the truth, for you see…" Before he could finish, a pork chop bone lodged in his throat. He gagged, coughed and expectorated, all in a most indecorous fashion. The woman offered no help, and within a minute he crumpled over and passed out of this world. The woman calmly finished her dinner, thinking all the while, "Well, at least he is no longer happy."

Moral: A paradox rejected is a paradox with fangs.

The Wolf and His Dupe

6. An agnostic, pondering the dilemma of unbelief, encountered a wolf caught in a steel trap. The wolf pleaded, "Won't you please set me free, kind sir? I am in terrible agony." "But how do I know that you won't eat me?" asked the agnostic. "You don't, of course. All I can give you is my word." The agnostic was reassured by the wolf's candor, and he disenthralled him from the trap. The wolf slouched at his feet in a show of gratitude. The agnostic felt that his dilemma had been resolved.

The wolf had other ideas. He sprang to his feet and promptly devoured his benefactor.

Moral: *Peril lurks outside the cloak of ignorance.*

The Cynic and the Simpleton

7. A cynic, walking in a vast field, was accosted by bandits. The bandits, finding the cynic penniless, proceeded to gouge out his eyes. A good-hearted simpleton, having witnessed the event, tried to comfort the cynic. "I'm sure you don't see it now but much good will come of this." The cynic responded, "I sure you are right, but it's bound to be lost in translation."

Moral: *An empty purse brings no good.*

The Huntsman and the Bear

8. A hunter came across a bear caught in a steel trap. "If you free me and give me a headstart, we will both enjoy the sport of a fine hunt." said the bear. The hunter was intrigued and began to pry open the jaws of the trap. The bear quickly disengaged its paw; but the trap was resistant and snapped shut, severing the hunters hands from his wrists. "Please go for help or I shall bleed to death," implored the hunter. "Most certainly, I will fetch a doctor." The bear, no longer requiring a headstart, lumbered slowly into the forest.

Moral: *A favor selfishly bestowed is a favor unhurriedly repaid.*

Death of a Mugwump

9. A Christian and a Latitudinarian were discussing a point of theology. The Christian asserted, "There is only one true religion, that of Jesus Christ, our Lord and Savior." The Latitudinarian replied, "I respect all religions and each sect within each religion. I accord a certain amount of truth to each." "That's just mush," retorted the Christian." A Muslin passing by and overhearing the conversation, screamed at the Christian, "Infidel! Allah is the only God and Islam the only true

religion." The Latitudinarian spoke softly, "You are both right after a fashion." The Christian and the Muslim, sensing a point of common ground, seized the Latitudinarian, tied him to a post and lit him aflame.

Moral: It is better to be a live fanatic than a dead chowderhead.

Late Blooming Flowers

10. A charming young lady once watched a darkly depressed young man from afar. Feeling intrigued, she approached him and inquired, "I sense that something is troubling you. May I take the liberty of asking you what it might be?" The young man replied disinterestedly, "Life is pointless; it's all for naught." "But do you not find the gorgeous flowers in that garden over there enchanting? He pondered, shook his head and slowly walked away. As he did so, he pondered some more. A short time later, they met by chance. He took her by the hand, and they walked away to plant a garden of their own.

Moral: Subsequent reflections may bring glorious results.

The Banker and the Beggar

11. A banker had just completed and enormously lucrative transaction in which he, using his talent for usury, had managed to defraud his rich client. As was leaving the bank, he was approached by a beggar. "Please kind sir, may I cadge a few pennies from you," pleaded the beggar. The banker, though miserly by nature, felt a sympathetic impulse. He reached inside his overcoat, fished out a twenty dollar bill and gave it to the beggar. "Bless you," said the vagabond. Now I have one more small favor to ask of you. May I walk with you for a spell, for I have a desire for some companionship?" The banker, annoyed by this odd request, sharply responded, "Away with you; you try my generosity!" The beggar, taking this as an affront to his dignity, took out a dagger and stabbed the banker in the back. He then slithered away into the night, after having relieved the banker of the rest of his funds. The beggar, taking this as an affront to his dignity, took out a dagger, and stabbed the banker in the back.

He then slithered away into the night, after having relieved the banker of the rest of his funds.

Moral: Miserliness of the heart is deadlier than that of the purse.

The Devil and the Atheist

12. A devil dressed in splendid fashion appeared to an atheist dressed in rags. Said the devil, "I will grant you anything you want in return for your soul." The atheist replied, "I do not believe you have the power to keep such a promise. However, if you will grant me a preliminary wish, I will agree to your proposal." "What is the wish?" asked the devil. To be dressed in fine clothes like yourself," said the atheist. In an instant, the devil had fulfilled the atheist's wish. The atheist reflected to himself, "This is a grand bargain for me, for I cannot lose what I do not have." Anxious to complete the deal, the atheist began, "You may have my soul and I wish for…" The devil grinned and interrupted, "Ah, and what a fine soul it is." As he turned to go, his prize in hand, he stopped and looked back at the atheist's rapidly decomposing body.

Moral: One may have more to lose than one thinks.

The Devil and the Wolf

13. A devil approached a wolf and said, "You have no soul for which we can bargain. However, I would still like to enlist your services as my chief lieutenant in the stealing of souls. In return, I proffer you treasure beyond your wildest dreams–gold, diamonds and endless feasting." The wolf bared its fangs and snarled, "Regarding the former, I have no use; as to the latter, I am a hunter nonpareil and can provide my own feasts. Besides, I am no stealer of souls." The devil, having nothing else to offer and fearing for his life, began gingerly to retreat The wolf leapt upon his interloper and ripped him to shreds.

Moral: The devil's bad bargain is the devil's demise.

The Pig and the Butcher

14. A farmer leading one of his pigs to the slaughterhouse crossed paths with a butcher on his way to his shop. The butcher said to the pig's owner, "That is a fine pig for which I will pay handsomely." The two reached a deal, and the butcher took charge of the pig. The butcher thought, "I will kill the pig before taking it to my shop." So thinking, the butcher drew forth his cleaver, raised it above his head and thrust it downward towards the pig's neck. The pig rolled over on its side and so managed to avoid the cleaver. The butcher took aim and again struck at the pig. The pig, though not quick, rolled back towards the butcher, escaping its death for the second time. It looked up at the butcher and squealed, then squealed again. The butcher thought, "This is a most unusual pig, clever enough to miss the cleaver and to plead for its life." Moved, he picked up the pig and carried it home.   For the next twenty years, the two remained inseparable companions. When the pig died, the butcher was grief-stricken. After a time though, he returned to his occupation of raising corn and alfalfa.

Moral: A change of heart brings blessed results.

The Donkey and the Driver

15. A donkey, pulling a load to market, gasped for air and came to a standstill. Its insensate and brutish driver leapt from his cart, hurling invectives at the poor beast. The uncomprehending donkey dropped to its knees unable to proceed. The driver, enraged by such obstinacy, began to lash him with a vengeance. A clan of highwaymen having espied the driver and his cart descended upon the scene. "Your money or your life," demand their leader. The driver pleaded, "I have no money, but please take my fruits and vegetables instead." The leader laughed, drew his pistol and shot the driver through the heart. They rode away, but one of the bandits returned and unleashed the donkey from the cart. The donkey rose and ambled on its way, leaving its owner and his wares to rot in the sun.

Moral: The cruelest of misdeeds is no match for a kind heart accompanied by a pistol.

The Judge and the Felon

16. A defendant convicted of a particularly heinous crime stood before the judge. "What have you to say for yourself?" asked the judge. "Nothing, I throw myself on the mercy of the court," replied the felon. "Very well, I have no choice but to sentence you to…" "Only this," interrupted the felon." "Do you believe in the principle that one should do unto others as one wants others to do unto oneself?" "Of course, the Golden Rule is a fine principle," said the judge. "Well then, would you want me to set you free if our situations were reversed?" asked the felon. The judge was flummoxed by this sophistry. He pondered for a moment and finally replied, "Why yes, that is exactly what I would want. I, therefore, grant you your freedom on one condition." "What is that," asked the felon. "That you never again appear in my court," said the judge. The felon walked out of the courtroom thinking, "That perversion of reasoning will likely not work on a smart judge." He applied it many times thereafter with the same result.

Moral: *Justice is best left to the wise.*

The Hawk and the Owl

17. A large hawk and a small owl pursued the same quarry, a tiny dormouse. The hawk swooped down just ahead of the owl and grasped the hapless dormouse. The owl said to the hawk, "You're a great predator, and such paltry game is unworthy of your prowess." The hawk was vain and replied to the owl, "You are correct," whereupon it dropped the mouse into the meadow. The owl made haste toward the dormouse, but the latter was faster and darted into its burrow, safely out of reach from the luckless owl. The hawk flew on its way and soon descried a large, dark form lumbering along the opposite side of the meadow. "Now there is a beast befitting my might," thought the hawk. It puffed out its chest and dove swiftly after its prey. Soon after, the hawk died of an infection incurred by one of the porcupine's quills.

Moral: *Our vanity often gives others the upper hand.*

The Katydid and the Streetlamp

18. A katydid, beckoned by a streetlamp, flew to within an inch of its death. The lure was irresistible, and the katydid crawled still closer. Then it turned and retreated a bit. The light was seductive, and the katydid again turned toward its executioner. A passerby witnessing this struggle cupped the katydid in her hand and laid it gently in the grass. The power of the light was not to be denied. The katydid flew up and landed on the lamp. The passerby softly removed the katydid and carried it to a dark spot yards away from The light. She walked on her way and never beheld the final act of the drama. The Next day the katydid was swallowed whole by a plump robin.

Moral: Nature brooks no interference.

The Woodsman and the Tree

19. A woodsman, ax in hand, prepared to fell a great tree. The tree spoke up, "Surely you realize that I am older than you and have seen a great deal more." The woodsman stepped back in disbelief. The tree continued, "I am much wiser than you. Don't do something which you are bound to regret." As the woodsman raised his ax, a bolt of lightning rent a thick branch from the tree which, in falling, crushed the woodsman.

"Yes," thought the tree. I have seen a great deal more."

Moral: The voice of nature is deadly for those who will not listen.

The Banquet of the Cicada Killers

20. A sacred burial ground, situated atop a grassy knoll, shimmered in the blazing summer heat. A man and a woman climbed to the top of the mound and beheld an eerie scene. At every step, a large wasp, known as a cicada killer, pinned to the ground a hapless cicada, draining its yellow blood. Fascinated, the woman knelt to closely observe one such murder. The wasp finished its meal and buzzed away in search of itsnext victim. The woman said to the man, "This is the weirdest thing I have ever seen?" They remained for a while transfixed by the mass carnage. Then they slowly descended the hill. That fall, heavy rains

pelted the mound burying the cicada skeletons in deep mud. They remained for a while transfixed by the mass carnage. Then they slowly descended the hill. That fall, heavy rains pelted the mound burying the cicada skeletons in deep mud.

Moral: The lore of ancient peoples persists in surrealistic places.

The Oracle and the Philosopher

21. An oracle, sitting in a cave lighted only by an eternal flame, was approached by a great philosopher. The philosopher asked the oracle, "What is the meaning of life?" She responded, "The answer you seek is to be found in asking yourself the right question. Ask it and you will know the answer to your original question." The philosopher, perplexed by the oracle's cryptic response, thought for a while. The same question repeatedly presented itself to him, and he asked it of himself. In a flash, he knew the answer to the question which had brought him to the oracle. He walked out of the cave, all the better for the two bits of wisdom gained.

Moral: The best knowledge lies hidden in what is already known.

The Cat in the Hookah Bar

22. One bitterly cold night, a stray cat crawled furtively through the slightly ajar door of a hookah bar. The cat was repelled by the thick, pungent smoke swirling from the hookahs; but the cat, having no better option, decided to stay. She quietly sought an inconspicuous nook by the fireplace. Unluckily for the cat, the owner discovered her and threw her back into the alley. A lonely vagabond picked her up and swaddled her in his filthy blanket. The two began a sad life together on the streets. After a time, the vagabond died of a lung infection. When the authorities showed up to dispose of his body, one of them noticed the cat, now an skeletal and pitiable figure. The man's eyes welled with tears. He hesitated as if uncertain as to what to do. Finally, he wrapped the cat in the vagabond's tattered blanket, took her to his home, named her Shisha and gave her a life befitting a princess.

Moral: Kindness takes many forms, all of them divine.

The Pauper at the Palace Door

23. A pauper got drunk on cheap wine. In a daze, he stumbled through the streets of the city and eventually collapsed unconscious before the door of a baronial manor. A party took place inside, and the owner's guests danced and grew giddy on fine spirits. When the festivities concluded, the merrymakers tumbled pell-mell their host's front door. Some of them noticed the pauper. They poked him, kicked him, laughed and continued on their way. A baron was the last reveler to leave. He was a different sort, philosophically disposed and not unkind of heart. He peered down at the fallen one, lifted him and hoisted him over his shoulder. He put him in his carriage and drove him to his estate. When the pauper awoke in the morning, the baron asked him, "And what account can you give of your sordid state?" "There is no accounting for such," answered the pauper. "A candid answer," said the baron. "You will make an interesting house guest. The pauper proved himself worthy of his host's belief; for he demonstrated a supple mind, keen wit and earnest gratitude. After a month, the host said to his guest, "It is time for you to go, but before you do, let me supply you with sufficient coin to make a new start in life. I know not of what it will avail you." The erstwhile pauper took the gift, left, and betook himself to the nearest tavern where he got drunk on fine wine and engaged the services of a strumpet. He pursued such a debauched and riotous life until he died, a pauper until the end

Moral: Good fortune dies in the soul of those who are powerless to accept it.

The Cobra and the Mongoose

24. A mongoose came across a cobra basking in the sun. "I am a cobra killer," said the mongoose. The uncomprehending cobra recoiled, and the mongoose advanced. "I shall dine on you before the sun has set," taunted the mongoose. The frightened cobra flared its hood and

delivered a strike missing the mongoose by a yard. "You pitiful creature," crowed the mongoose. "My mission is even easier than I thought." The aggressor moved even closer, and the cobra struck furiously, missing its target. The mongoose lunged repeatedly, easily avoiding the strikes of the hapless cobra. Finally, the exhausted serpent collapsed to the ground. The mongoose moved in for the kill. The cobra mustered a wild and desperate final strike, piercing the jugular of its adversary. The mongoose convulsed and fell dead before its prey. The cobra, unaware of its near death escape, crawled sluggishly away in search of toads, rodents and other food.

Moral: Overconfidence seldom wins the day.

The Miser and the Doctor

25. A miser fell ill. He beckoned his servant and said, "Go and fetch that thief of a doctor: have him come at once." The servant obeyed and brought back the doctor. He entered the sick man's bedroom to find him lying on his bed beneath a moth-eaten quilt. "Ah, we're feeling a bit under the weather are we," said the doctor. The miser snapped, "I have no time for pleasantries; just give me some medicine." He then offered the apothecary a small silver coin. "Very well, but for such a paltry sum, this is the best I can do." He handed the miser a small vial filled with a red liquid. "Drink this and you will feel better by tomorrow morning." He drank the liquid and fell asleep. He awoke the next morning only to find his condition markedly worse. "Go again and bring me that quacksalver," he screeched at his servant. The doctor came again, and the miser offered him a small gold coin and received a vial filled with a blue liquid. The miser drank the liquid and fell asleep, but this elixir proved even less roborant than the first. He awoke the next morning on the brink of death. The doctor was summoned for a third time. The dying man said faintly, "I am afraid it is too late." "Nonsense, I have hear my most potent remedy. It's guaranteed to fully restore your health, but you must pay a princely sum for it." The miser offered two gold pieces. The doctor scoffed and said, "Your stinginess

insults me, but I am of a generous heart today. He gave his patient a vial filled with a gold liquid. The miser drank it, convulsed violently and died. The doctor said to the servant, "There, the deed is done. Unfasten the key from his belt so that we may open his strongbox and split his fortune". The servant gave a sinister grin, pulled a pistol from his master's coat and shot the doctor through the heart. He then did as he had been told only to find that the box contained only sand. Soon after, the murderer was apprehended and hanged. The authorities left his body to sway from the gallows, where it was soon picked clean by the resident rooks.

Moral: Greed has no winners.

The Old Man's Inquisitor

26. An old man who had lived and upright life, or at least so he would have told you, was taking his dinner at his favorite cafe. He lingered over his wine. As he took his last sip, he was surprised to see a shadowy, masked figure sitting across the table from him. "And do what do I owe the pleasure?" he asked his interlocutor. The visitor ignored the question and asked in his turn, "Do you remember that night when you found a scrawny and bedraggled kitten, took her in and raised her to a beautiful and grateful companion?" "Why yes," he replied in amazement. "But how can you know that? I have never seen you before." The stranger again disregarded the question and queried, "And your wife, the one who worshiped you to a fault, but to whom you showed little gratitude or affection, do you remember her?" "Yes, of course, but I resent…" The interrogator drew close to the old man's face and looked accusingly at him through glowing coal-eyes. He continued his line of questioning. "Do you recall your many friends– some of whom you treated with compassion and respect, but others whom you cheated and traduced behind their backs? Then there was the time when a drug-ravaged streetwalker asked you for money for food; but you, suspecting she wanted it for drugs, offered her only a homily on sin and implored her to repent before God?" "But I never…

" the old man broke off trembling. "Who… who are you?" His inquisitor for the first time responded, "I am everyone and I am no one." He then dislimned leaving behind him only a horrible black and rose mask. The old man slipped seamlessly into oblivion.

Moral: There is no ambit between life and death, no discrete moment upon which we may dwell.

Two Fiends and a Goddess

27. Two murderers sat on a riverbank discussing their long history of crime. The first one boasted, "I once accosted a gentleman and demanded of him his money. He readily complied. I then, for no particular reason, shot him in cold-blood." The second one remarked, "Ah, an impressive misdeed, heinous and unnecessary. I sense in you a commendable amorality. "But in that regard, I have no equal. I once kidnapped a wealthy heiress and demanded of her father a huge ransom. I promised him the safe return of his daughter if he acceded. Of course, I had no intention of honoring my promise. Now I knew quite well the path he would take to deliver the ransom. I waited concealed behind a bush. As he passed along the road, I leapt forth and jugulated him with my dagger. I watched in glee as the blood ran down his chest. I pocketed the ransom and ran back to his daughter's place of confinement intending to submit her to the same fate. However, when I arrived, I found that she had escaped. Damn that brat, I thought; she has denied me a second pleasure." As the two sat engaged in recounting their grisly crimes, a strange figure clad in a diaphanous gown, emerged from the river, made her way up the bank and sat down between the two criminals. Sensing a lucky opportunity, they withdrew their poniards and stabbed her through the heart, but no blood spurted forth. Their weapons met with all the resistance of mist on a rainy day. She rose, made her way back down the bank and disappeared into the water. Enraged, the fiends turned on each other. In an instant, both lay dead upon the ground, each drenched in the blood of the other.

Moral: An evil soul begets its own end, an end both horrible and just.

Flying Away with the Truth

28. Two dogmatists confronted each other crossing a narrow bridge. The first roared, "Stand aside; I am for truth and justice and will have my way." The second stiffened and parried, "Back down you blackguard, for my truths are greater than yours." Each lunged helplessly at the other, missed and fell to their deaths in the dark waters below. A raven, amused at the ignominious result of this dispute, swooped low over the water, croaked, and flew upon its carefree way.

Moral: An unexpected encounter with the truth is a breath of fresh air.

The Ghost of the Lion

29. One night on a lonely savannah, a pride of lionesses was devouring a freshly killed gazelle, but the night here is merciless, and the lionesses soon found themselves encircled by a pack of vicious hyenas. A life and death struggle was imminent. The pride, hopelessly outnumbered, found themselves at the mercy of its interlopers. Of a sudden, the outlying brush parted and a massive lion, black mane whipping in the wind, charged, and scattered the hyenas. He brought down a straggler, savaging its jugular. He is… the hyena killer. Soon after, a begrimed jeep carrying poachers invaded this drama. They proceeded to shoot down the brave lion. Finding nothing marketable in the thoughtlessly slain lion, they drove away into the night. The next morning the bloody, laniated bodies of the poachers were discovered not far from their muddy jeep.

Moral: The struggle between life and death comes full circle.

The Cheetah and the Zebra

30. A zebra grazed peacefully on the African savannah. A cheetah, not fifty feet away, bolted across the plain and leapt for the zebra's neck. The zebra bucked and threw off the cheetah.

Undeterred, the cheetah leapt again, this time catching the brunt of the zebra's hoof. The stunned cheetah backed away, paused, and reflected.

The cheetah said, "You are a fine and courageous specimen. Let us become friends, and I will protect you from dangerous predators; for your part, you will…" The zebra interrupted, braying condescendingly. "From such feckless adversaries as yourself?" Rebuffed for a second time, the cheetah slunk away in disgrace. Soon after, three hyenas accomplished what the cheetah could not.

Moral: Never reject a proffered alliance out of arrogance.

The Vulture and the Leopard

31. A vulture, engaged in the consumption of a decomposing warthog, was confronted by a leopard.

The vulture, sensing the imminent loss of its meal, entreated the leopard, "It is but carrion upon which I dine. You prefer live game. Please let me finish my meal." "Certainly" answered the leopard in an obliging tone. The vulture proceeded to pick clean the bones of the warthog. "Thank you; I am most grateful." said the vulture. Whereupon, the leopard sprang upon the bird, quickly dispatching it with a well-placed bite. "Ugh," cried the leopard as he bit into the vulture. "This flesh is putrid." He then left, leaving his prey to rot in the sun—a tasty meal for other vultures.

Moral: De gustibus non est disputandum: There is no disputing about taste.

The Traveler's Lament

32. A wandering profligate passed a ramshackle house of ill-repute. Outside, some clients peed on the walls and defecated in the grass. A slattern covered in boils emerged from inside and approached the traveler. Said she, "For a few pence, we shall have our fun." He agreed. Not long after, he developed syphilis and went blind. One night while groping his way along a path, he tripped over some exposed roots, fell into a river, and drowned.

Moral: Blindness comes too soon for the lost.

The Small Hawk and the Eagle

33.An unprepossessing hawk said to a majestic eagle, "You are the symbol of great nations, but you subsist on carrion, while I am disparaged far and wide for snatching a few hens. The ways of the world are not fair." The eagle, unimpressed, struck the head of the hawk with its mighty talons. The hawk fell limply to the ground. A few days later, the eagle returned to the spot and carried off the carcass of the objector.

Moral: *Nature makes no allowance for morality.*

The Stray in the Blizzard

24.One night a blizzard came upon the earth. The temperature plunged below zero, and blinding snow ripped through fields and forests. It lashed the ice-covered windows of homes and tall buildings. Engulfed in Nature's fury, a lost soul wandered looking for shelter—shelter not to be had. Ice crystals formed on her matted coat of the wanderer, and her breath became halting. Her gait became staggered and slow. Death loomed. But Fortune is not always unkind. At last she found herself on the patio of a modest dwelling. The owner of the home, by chance or miracle, happened to look out the window and catch sight of the lost one. The owner opened the door and by word and gesture bade her come in. She backed away, trembling. "Come," said the owner softly, "It's alright." She said nothing, but labored through the snow and into the home. The owner wrapped her in a blanket and asked, "What is your name?" She opened her mouth to answer, but no sound escaped. "It doesn't matter; I shall call you…"

Moral: *Every stray should have a name.*

The Bee, the Bear and the Queen

35. A bee carrying its pollen to its hive was eaten by a swallow. A second pollen-carrying bee met the same fate. A third bee was more fortunate. However, it lost a wing in its effort to avoid the swallow and fell to the ground. The bee was nothing if not hardy and devoted, and it was able to return to the hive with its cargo. The queen said to her loyal bearer, "Why are you so late, you sluggard?" "I have no excuse your

majesty except that unfortunate circumstances have delayed me." "Bah!" scoffed the queen. "To the devil with you and your circumstances." She unceremoniously pierced him with her giant mandibles and lapped his crimson blood. As she drank, a ravenous bear stumbled upon the hive. With a swooping stroke of it giant paw, the bear ripped open the hive and devoured its contents, queen and all.

Moral: Alas, loyalty and gratitude are no match for the mighty.

Four Bandits and a Sheriff

36. Three highwaymen, having pulled off a nice bit of knavery, returned to their leader with their booty. The leader said, "I will divide these gold coins equally among us." "A capital idea exclaimed the other three miscreants." But one of them glared balefully at the leader. He fancied himself the mastermind of the theft. No sooner had the leader started to divvy out the coins, when he drew his poniard and stabbed him through the heart. "Now," said he, "We'll each have a third." "Here, here!" shouted the others, but even as they rejoiced, one of them drew his pistol and shot the mastermind to death. "Even better," clapped both. "A half is better than a third." Each eyed the other suspiciously. The shooter quickly drew his pistol, but the other was too fast. He grabbed the sack of gold and threw it at his adversary, crushing his skull. He retrieved the sack and began to make his escape. However, he had not gone two steps before he was surrounded by a sheriff and his posse. The sheriff laughed heartily. "We shall have a fine spectacle in our village tomorrow. This rogue shall dangle from our gibbet. Afterwards, I will apportion the contents of this bag equally among our townspeople.

Moral: Equality attended by greed makes for deadly foes.

The Relativist and the Absolutist

37. A relativist and an absolutist engaged in an arcane truth! regarding the nature of truth. The relativist said, "All truth is relative. It depends on the perspective of the individual or the society." The

absolutist fumed, "That's nonsense, the theory of a mushhead. All truth is universal." Both presented clever arguments for their position, but the debate reached an impasse. Neither budged an inch. The absolutist finally proposed a demonstration. "Come, let us ascend to the top of the skyscraper which towers above us." The relativist willingly obliged. Upon reaching the top, the absolutist prodded the relativist onto the ledge. "Now jump! I guarantee, absolutely, that you will fall." The relativist refused. The absolutist bellowed in triumph, "Ah, your reluctance to accept my challenge decisively proves my point." In his joy, he jumped up entangling his feet with his adversary. Both plummeted from the ledge onto the pavement below. The absolutist landed first and died a gruesome death. The relativist landed atop the absolutist, unharmed.

Moral: Whosoever wins the argument may be the biggest loser.

The Woman and Her Timid Cat

38. A woman went out one morning to inspect her garden. She was greeted by soft mews. Looking around, she discovered a beautiful black and white kitten. She picked up the kitten, cradled him to her breast, and took him into her house. The woman was kind and made to the kitten many overtures of affection; but the kitten was shy and scared, unable to accept the offers. The kitten remained with the woman and led a good life, eating gourmet foods and lying on plush Persian rugs. He developed the curious habit of constantly mewing, mewing when he wanted his food, his toys, mewing just to mew. The woman named him Mewster. For many years, sixteen in all, this improbable relationship, woman and cat maintaining a respectful distance, continued. Eventually, the cat grew ill and scrannel. One evening as the woman lay watching television, Mewster crawled into her bed and showered her with love. The next morning the woman awoke to find Mewster draped across her arm, limp and barely responsive. She rushed him to the vet. There, on the advice of the doctor and in an act of kindness, she had him put to sleep. She had Mewster cremated and his

remains sealed in a wooden urn. When the urn was returned to the woman, she noticed on its lid the engraving 'Mewfster,' a cruel misspelling of her friend's name.

Moral: Love may lie hidden in the heart.

The World as It Is

39. In a dingily lit bar, several small groups of customers sat at formica tables haphazardly scattered around the floor. At the bar, other patrons, mostly men, sat on worn stools. These men were as much a fixture of the place as the stale cigarette smoke which hung in the air. Two of the men were engaged in a debate, a debate which replayed itself for the umphteenth time, in this bar and many others throughout time. One animatedly pressed his view and the other languidly responded. Both were so unprepossessing that except for their marked difference in demeanor and height, no one would have bothered to tell them apart. The short, animated one gestured and sputtered as if the outcome of their argument was a matter of life and death; the tall, languid one stretched and yawned as if preparing for a nap. Neither of them noticed—nor did anyone else—the entrance of a young man through the bar's side door. The man paused for a moment and surveyed the odd tableau which confronted him. His eyes flitted nervously. He took a hesitant step forward and then another step back. He turned as if to go, but the two polemicists caught his attention. He wasn't sure why, but the theatrics of the short one determined him to stay. He walked over to the bar and took a stool next to the object of his interest. Neither debater paid him any mind. He looked intently at the pair. There was disgust and puzzlement in his gaze; disgust for the short, animated one and puzzlement for the tall, languid one. Finally, the former took notice of the young man and remarked, "Ah, fine sir, perhaps you can settle a point of disputation between my friend and me. He then proceeded to recount the substance of his argument. "You see, I'm certain that the world is governed by a divine Providence which, even in the most trying circumstances, intercedes to bring about the best

possible results. The ways of Providence are sometimes hard to fathom and contrary to observations of particular incidents. However, an understanding of the whole state of affairs brings clearly to light the veridicality of this view." The young man fidgeted, fumbling with an object in his coat pocket. "What are your views on the subject?" he asked the other. "Everything which happens happens by chance and random circumstance. We are at the mercy of a chaotic and unpredictable world. Even the most prescient of plans are likely all for naught." The young man became visibly more agitated, shifting his glance from the two disputants to the other habitues of the bar. Finally, he composed himself and drew a small revolver from his coat pocket. "Now I shall take all of your money, as well as the money from everyone present." He did so while the optimist whispered to his companion, "He will take our money, leave us unharmed, and depart with our funds. Soon, thereafter, he will be arrested by the police and our money will be returned to us. The robber turned to leave, lingered for a moment and then, with a sure aim, he shot the optimist dead. As fate would have it, a gendarme was passing by the bar. He apprehended the murderer. Soon after, the money was returned to the tall, languid man and its other rightful owners.

Moral: By Chance or by Providence, it cannot be said; for the ways of the Universe cannot be read.

The Lawyer and Her Client

40. A high-ranking executive at a prestigious company was accused of embezzlement. The firm had incontrovertible evidence to prove its case. Faced with the dim prospect of acquittal, the executive enlisted the services of a renowned lawyer with an unimpeachable record in such cases. The accused met with his lawyer. "Are you guilty?" she asked. "No," said her client. "You're lying, but that is irrelevant," said the lawyer. "All that matters is a favorably disposed jury and my presentation. Of the latter, I am certain. The former is probable as well." The case went to trial. After much chaffering among the lawyers, the jurors were selected. A logician and a scientist were among the prospective jurors. The defendant's lawyer

was successful in ensuring that neither of them made the cut. She smiled at her client; the battle was half won. The plaintiff presented an airtight case. But the defendant's lawyer was up to the challenge. With unrivaled aplomb, she cited the defendant's community service, his position of deacon in his church, his love of family, his battle with cancer, and many other points not germane to the case. The jurors, visibly moved, adjourned, and a minute later returned with a verdict of not guilty.

Moral: Logic and substance are no match for style and panache.

The One-eyed Cat and the Gambler

41. A starving, one-eyed cat roamed a dark alley looking for food. Having no luck, the cat stopped and laid down. He thought, "I have no food and no strength to go on. I will surely die here tonight." It began to utter a series of pitiful mews when it noticed a ray of light falling aslant through the slightly ajar door of a building abutting the alley. "I have nothing to lose," thought the cat. With great effort, he raised himself and walked through the door. The building was a gambling den. Around one of the tables sat several men playing poker. One of the men was in the midst of a terrible run of bad luck. He was about to play his final hand when the cat crawled over and rubbed around his leg. He looked down and exclaimed, "Ah, a black cat come to double my rotten luck." He kicked the cat to the side, played his hand and won. The cat came back and laid limply across his boot. Not noticing the cat, he played again and again, winning every time. He finally looked down and saw the cat. "Whoa, what is this, a prince of a cat come to win me a fortune." He gently picked up the cat, cradled him to his breast, and took him home. He served him a sumptuous meal of cream, turkey, and other assorted viands. It was the first of a million such meals for the one-eyed cat.

Moral: Persistence and a touch of luck make for good fortune.

www.ingramcontent.com/pod-product-compliance
Lightning Source LLC
Chambersburg PA
CBHW071328150726
47997CB00002B/642